PENGUIN BOOKS

THREE LETTERS FROM THE ANDES

Patrick Leigh Fermor was born in 1915 of English and Irish descent. After a 'stormy' school career and his year-and-a-half journey on foot to Constantinople, he lived and travelled in the Balkans and the Greek Archipelago. During that time he acquired a deep interest in languages and a love of remote places. He joined the Irish Guards in 1939 and the 'I' Corps in 1941, became liaison officer in Albania and fought in Greece and Crete, to which, during the German occupation, he returned three times (once by parachute). Disguised as a shepherd, he lived for over two years in the mountains, organizing the resistance and the capture and evacuation of the German Commander, General Kreipe. He was awarded the DSO in 1944 and the OBE in 1943, and was made Honorary Citizen of Herakleion, Crete. Patrick Leigh Fermor has also written *The Traveller's Tree*, about the West Indies, which won the Heinemann Foundation Prize for Literature in 1950 and the Kemsley Prize in 1951, *A Time to Keep Silence*, *The Violins of Saint Jacques*, *Mani*, winner of the Duff Cooper Memorial Prize and a Book Society Choice, and its companion volume, *Roumeli*, and *A Time of Gifts* (Penguin), winner of the 1978 W. H. Smith & Son Annual Literary Award and the 1992 Prix Audiberti de la Ville d'Antibes, described by Jan Morris as 'nothing short of a masterpiece', which covers his exacting journey to Constantinople, as far as Hungary. The sequel, *Between the Woods and the Water*, continues the story of this journey. It won the 1987 Thomas Cook Travel Book Award and the Silver Pen Award. Many of these books are published by Penguin. Patrick Leigh Fermor now lives in Greece in a house he designed and built. He is a visiting member of the Athens Academy, has been awarded the Gold Medal of Honour of the Municipality of Athens and is Hon. D. Litt. at the University of Kent.

PATRICK LEIGH FERMOR

———————

THREE LETTERS
FROM THE ANDES

PENGUIN BOOKS

PENGUIN BOOKS

Published by the Penguin Group
Penguin Books Ltd, 27 Wrights Lane, London W8 5TZ, England
Penguin Books USA Inc., 375 Hudson Street, New York, New York 10014, USA
Penguin Books Australia Ltd, Ringwood, Victoria, Australia
Penguin Books Canada Ltd, 10 Alcorn Avenue, Toronto, Ontario, Canada M4V 3B2
Penguin Books (NZ) Ltd, 182–190 Wairau Road, Auckland 10, New Zealand

Penguin Books Ltd, Registered Offices: Harmondsworth, Middlesex, England

First published by John Murray (Publishers) Ltd 1991
Published in Penguin Books 1992
1 3 5 7 9 10 8 6 4 2

Printed in England by Clays Ltd, St Ives plc

For Debo and Andrew

DRAWINGS BY JOHN CRAXTON

Note

THIS was a private account of an Andean journey organized and led by Robin Fedden in 1971. As I had no particular task during the journey, except looking after the Primus stove, I wrote down a rough and ready description of our doings in the form of three long letters to my wife Joan in Greece, the last of which was never posted as I finished it in the plane just before we landed in England. I've cut out one or two irrelevant passages, topped and tailed it a bit, but not much, and generally tidied it up to make it more presentable as a sort of memento of the journey.

P.L.F.
Messenia, Greece, 1991

'*He has written a slim volume on Hittite ivories.*'
'*There are no Hittite ivories.*'
'*That is why the volume is so slim.*'
Imaginary Conversations

First Letter

First Letter

AT last the morning of departure arrived in Little Venice,[1] but no sign of the ordered car. We dialled and dialled for a cab, everywhere was engaged, so in despair I began lugging my stuff to the pavement while Patrick Kinross[2] stood in the middle of Warwick Avenue in his Persian silk dressing-gown imperiously waving and to some purpose. A taxi stopped at once.

I needn't have worried, as it drew up at Victoria Air Terminal at the same instant as Andrew's,[3] and we were the first arrivals. He was wearing a pink pullover and a white linen hat and both of us were clumping about already shod in our climbing boots, clutching ice-axes like tomahawks. We're the two beginners, the weak links in the chain, and anxious to make a good impression.

The others arrived a bit later: Robin and Renée[4] and then André Choremi. He's a cousin of all the other Choremis in

[1] London, W2
[2] Lord Kinross, writer and historian
[3] Duke of Devonshire MC
[4] Robin Fedden, author, poet, traveller, Deputy Director-General Historical Buildings, National Trust, and his wife, Renée, were the leaders of the expedition.

3

Greece and Egypt, but they have been French since Dela-croix's *Massacre of Chios*, I think. He's a lawyer and a social anthropologist, lives in Provence and speaks perfect English and we had met ages ago with Julian Pitt-Rivers. Then Carl Natar turned up, who is Swiss, and equally at home in French, English, German and Italian, besides his mother-tongue which—a specimen of wonderful rarity—is Romanche, and he comes from the same valley in the Engadine as Gia-cometti. He is a great climber, an ex-world ski champion, I think; and he was the London manager of Cartiers for thirty years. He is also one of two identical twins. The seventh member of the party is Myles Hildyard, a Nottinghamshire squire; he was coming to Lima with us on the way to visit his brother, who is Ambassador in Chile. He's an old mountain hand and it's a pity he's not accompanying us to the Andes. They are all delightful. Our stuff—rucksacks, kitbags, tents and other climbing gear—formed an enormous pyramid in the Departure Lounge.

The chartered plane was full of fellow-members of the Andean Society, all bent on tackling various South American ranges and up to the eyes in equipment; there was also a small party of scientists bound for the Galapagos Islands. I sat between Renée and Myles and we chatted and read and snoozed and ate—meals, snacks, coffee, drinks and sandwiches appeared to arrive non-stop—as the West Country roared away underneath us, and then the Atlantic. Myles was with a Yeomanry regiment in the Battle of Crete. I extracted the description of how he escaped after capture, with Cretan help, and finally got away in a small boat to Asia Minor and back to his unit. At about midday—almost at once, it seemed—we landed in Bermuda and drank a planter's punch in the

airport bar; then flew on to Antigua—*Traveller's Tree*[1]
country. We could just see St Kitts and the Windward Islands
to the north, and to the south, the ghosts of Guadeloupe and
Dominica. One engine had gone wrong, so we were stuck
here for six hours until at last, after a dozen false alarms and
re-embarkations, a new plane was flown from Trinidad. We
were now in the small hours of the following day by London
time, but it was only early evening in our new hemisphere.

Night had fallen when we started the last flight to Lima,
so we saw none of the Leeward isles and no Amazonian
forests, and no Andes. We were flying away from the sun,
and by the time we staggered down the steps into Lima
airport in the small hours, we had been travelling nearly
twenty-four hours. The passport and currency formalities
took a long time. The sleepy, rather blank-faced half-Indian
officials were far from brisk; our passports seemed to puzzle
them and Andrew's proved utterly enigmatic. He got through
the last barrier half an hour after they'd finished with the rest
of us, murmuring sadly: 'I can't deny there *are* countries
where being a duke is a bit of an advantage; but Peru's
not one of them.' Our scattered gear, when it was finally
assembled, counted, re-counted and wheeled out by four
straining peons, filled an entire taxi. We drove after it in
another into dark, damp Lima, staggered to our rooms in the
Alcazar Hotel like seven phantoms and dropped into oblivion.

We all had to double up, so Andrew and I shared rooms.
He's much tidier than I am, but I plan to improve.

I'm dazzled by Robin's quiet and imperturbable com-

[1] My account of a journey through the Caribbean Islands (published
1950)

petence in the management of the whole undertaking: never a hint of fuss, impatience or strain. Pleasure is the watchword and it tinges all our doings with comedy and charm.

*　　　*　　　*

We woke to the clang of marches and military bands. Speeches were booming non-stop from a score of loudspeakers in honour of Peru's National Day. (A military regime is in power, left-orientated but superficially indistinguishable from other military regimes.)

It is midwinter in South America, and drizzle was falling. Except for about sixty days a year, Lima is permanently overcast, and mist, clouds and spindrift are borne everlastingly inland by the Humboldt Current. The town is a terrible mess, but here and there the skyscrapers give way to wooden *miradors* and *rejas* and Jesuit barley-sugar columns and Counter-Reformation saints: the cloisters, domes, cupolas and belfries are swamped in development but they show what a beautiful town it must once have been. We had luncheon in a fine Spanish colonial house with Sr. and Sra. Porros, who are grand, Anglophile and kind; then we trooped round the gardens of Mr Tweedie, a great botanist and horticulturist, who has gathered innumerable rare specimens from all over the world and lives in a house full of books and pictures. We were still half-stunned with sleep and everyone chucked dinner except Myles, André and me. This involved us in a wild-goose chase through a maze of backstreets in search of a fish restaurant called El Pescador, where we ate shrimps and *loup-de-mer*; it was close to an eerie, rather intriguing-looking late-Victorian-Gothic castle called the Castello Rospigliosi.

6

Wc got up at 5.30 a.m., drove to the airport and climbed into a little Peruvian plane belonging to the inauspiciously named Fawcett Line. It carried us up into the mist and out over the Pacific coast, which was a line of steep brown cliffs beetling over grey waves. White clouds swallowed us up; but when the plane turned inland and climbed into the sunshine, a new world began. The foothills of the Andes were floating like islands on an ocean of cloud. The mountains soon cohered in a moleskin-coloured massif with rivers of cloud penetrating the ravines and hanging over the ledges like frozen waterfalls. Villages and fields and cattle-folds died away. Empty plateaux, gleaming with pools, ascended to snow-powdcred conical mountains and soon patterns of snow were piling up along all their southern flanks. (North is South here, the compass is reversed.) Beyond thc next cloud-line rose a sierra of peaks and table mountains and giant staircases and canyons along which the clouds floated like strings of tennis-balls. A taller range loomcd, and we caught glimpses of the sea of cloud that covers the western fringes of the Amazon basin. At some point we must have crossed a watershed, for all the torrent-beds gleaming at the bottom of dark valleys began to point in a different direction. A flashing line of glaciers rose, creased and curled between bare peaks that were too steep for the snow to settle and faraway dim cordilleras floated on the blue vapour. Then the unwinding began. A few saffron-coloured fields appeared, and, as we lost height, patches of ploughland, rough walls, channels, farms, cows, poplars, and at last the domes and the belfries of Cuzco. We landed in a small aerodrome full of Quechua Indians.

*   *   *

We all feel breathless, racked with headaches and weak at the knees. We have been whisked from sea-level to a height of 11,000 feet in the space of an hour. This malaise must be the revenge of the Children of the Sun on the co-sectaries of the Conquistadors. We creep about the streets in dark glasses and shady hats. The glare is blinding, the shade cool and sunset icy.

The little Conquistador Hotel, run by a dark mestizo and manned by a staff of squat, dark, smiling Quechua Indians, overlooks the Indian market, and market-noises sail in through the windows. A railway runs down the middle of the street outside, and at dusk a Puffing Billy hoots and clangs along it like a prairie train in a film. The neighbouring houses are low and ramshackle, built of earth and adobe, but nearer the heart of the town Spanish buildings spring out of megalithic walls which are the remains of the Inca temples and palaces. There are two splendid plazas and a score of baroque churches abound in spiral columns, broken pediments, pyramids and obelisks. Pinnacled arches span the streets and the streets themselves tilt uphill, like diving-boards into the sky, or end at stupendous churches or steep mountainsides. The Andes surround the city. The earthquake-stricken palaces of noblemen and archbishops, the intricate woodwork, the wide eaves and the thin air remind me of Kathmandu; there's the same balance of richness and squalor, only with churches instead of temples and Quechua Indians replacing the Nepalese and the Tibetans, whose bronze faces theirs slightly resemble. The women wear multicoloured woollen shawls and carry papooses on their backs. Their long, raven plaits are crowned with bowler-hats or white and slightly tapering straw toppers and they squat along the kerbs over pyramids of yam, potato,

8

maize, grass provender and heaps of enigmatic edible pods. The fact that they never walk but always seem to trot gives a feeling of scuttling urgency to the narrow lanes. White woolly dogs scamper everywhere. It is a remarkable town, and we long to explore it.

We took to our beds at five, resurrected at eight for some soup, then retired again with sleeping draughts at nine and slept flat out. We feel a bit better today; but we're far from acclimatized. The briefest walk is exhausting; one is short of breath, hearts pound and heads throb with dazzle and vertigo and straightening up again after tying a shoelace seems a Herculean task.

Later on

Except for Andrew and Carl, we all felt pretty mouldy still as we tramped through Inca megaliths, palaces of colonial grandees and vast Jesuit interiors. (These are ablaze with gilt, crowded with scourgings and martyrdoms and peopled by Virgins dressed like Mary Queen of Scots in black and gold robes crusted with stars, and bleeding hearts radiate swords. Indian women with their bowlers doffed kneel in the twinkling gloom in near-ecstasy. There is gold and blood everywhere.) Returning, we slump cataleptically on our beds.

Four old Inca ruins are scattered in the hills above Cuzco, commanding airy vistas of mountain and ravine with tinkling streams and small troops of llamas grazing among the giant walls. The largest of these, Sacsayhuaman, is one of the most impressive bits of fortification I've ever seen. The colossal leaning zigzags are built of granite blocks, some of them

9

weighing many tons; one of these is twenty feet high and all of them are irregular in shape but so beautifully slotted together that (as no one fails to say) you couldn't insert a knife-blade between them. Much of Cuzco itself is built in this Cyclopean style; it still has the layout of the old pre-Conquest city and whole streets of leaning blocks ascend many feet before their giant masonry skilfully merges into Spanish architecture.

I'm sorry to have missed a visit to the ruins of Pisac, sixty miles away. (I stayed behind to scribble these slapdash pages before I forget.) The others came back with such tales of giant architectural wreckage, desolate highland scenery and multicoloured costumes in the Indian market that I'm gnawed with envy.

The llamas have conquered all hearts. They have even longer eyelashes than Robin. How does a llama answer in Spanish, if you ask what he's called?

'*¿Como se llama?*'

'*¡Llama!*'

* * *

We set off on August 1 for Machu Picchu, hoping to hurry on our acclimatization, as it is two thousand feet lower than Cuzco, but still nine thousand above sea-level. The little train lifted us slowly out of the basin in which Cuzco lies in a sequence of switchbacks up the mountain, and then the track ran straight across a plateau with little vegetation except the universal eucalyptus and the willows that lined the many streams; then it tilted into the gorge down which the Urubamba river flows. It became richer and more varied with every mile. Organ-cactus, yucca and maguey were replaced by tree-ferns, balisier, flame-trees and trees with large mauve flowers; breadfruit and pawpaw followed, then really tall forest bruisers sprang up, like those in the Petén jungle, all of them tufted with parasites and strung with lianas. The scene changed fast as we sank from layer to layer until at last we were in a sub-tropical forest filled with bamboo, mare's-tail, brilliant flowers, butterflies, egrets, clouds of wood-pigeons and flights of green parakeets bursting from the leaves. The blue-green Urubamba river meanwhile (which flows into the Marañon and then into the Amazon) rushed tumbling through thousands of tall, white Henry Moore-like boulders which millennia of current had polished smooth. Sometimes the masonry of overgrown Inca embankments stretched intact along the brink, and sometimes, in little riverside clearings, prehistoric-looking hamlets of stone and thatch assembled and the old Inca highway climbed at a slant across the mountains.

At the station under Machu Picchu, a tall and striking figure with a shaven head and a face of great benignity was waiting to ascend. His brown knee-length habit was caught in at the waist above bare and sturdy legs and criss-cross sandals. His plaited wicker hat was a shallow hemisphere half a yard across inscribed with columns of Japanese ideograms and he carried a tall polished staff with an intricate silver emblem at the top. This was a Zen Buddhist monk from an abbey near Yokohama, travelling light on a solitary pilgrimage around the world. It was the Eightfold Path that had brought him to the Andes.

A zigzag track lifted us to Machu Picchu. The place stands on a spike of mountain made for eagles, linked by a saddle to another great sweep of the mountain and dominating a labyrinth of gorges and answering spikes. The Urubamba, now, rushes along the bottom of a dark and echoing abyss two thousand feet below and its roar is always in our ears.

In the evening, when tourists had melted away, we wandered about the ruins: a hushed, mysterious place of giant and hermetically-fitting geometric stones, many times the size of Mycenae and Tyrins. The courtyards, staircases and terraces diminish in a geometry of ledges to smaller parallelograms on which chambers, sacrificial stones and temples are built. They culminate in a platform once used as a sundial. The doors and windows and niches are trapezoidal, isosceles triangles, that is, cut off halfway up. The place has the atmosphere of Copán in Honduras without the decoration, for everything is grimly functional here: a secret palace and fortress far from Spanish ears and eyes, where the Incas lived on for ages after the arrival of the Conquistadors; and it was only discovered and hacked out of the oblivion of the forests sixty years ago. As the sun set, we walked a little way along the old Inca road which used to run from Machu Picchu to Cuzco. (Robin suggested that relays of fleet-footed Indians used to rush live lobsters from the coast far below for the emperor's banquets.) Much is effaced and overgrown, and in the undergrowth, beside a ruined guard-post or staging-point, we found a few marvellous giant yellow orchids, growing as large as daffodils on the tips of bamboo-like stalks six feet high. (Carl and Andrew laboriously hacked up the tangled roots of one of them next day with a kitchen knife. It is to be replanted in the new conservatory at Chatsworth, and if it takes, we'll all get cuttings or bulbs.) I wonder if they found lots of new species when Hiram Bingham, the discoverer of the ruins, started hacking the jungle back in

1911? He sounds a fascinating man; the uncle, I think, of Henrietta Bingham, Carrington's friend.

It is a lonely, hushed, mythical place of unforgettable beauty, severity and strangeness. The dusk deepened as we returned. We looked down on the green rectangular ledges of terrace, geometrically diminishing like lawns, as they rose in tiers from the great central parade-ground. Shadowy llamas grazed on them. We heard faint cries and laughter below, where three little Quechua boys were playing football in the dark; the invisible ball thumped and bounced among the Cyclopean walls.

Joined to the ruins by a narrow hammock-like causeway, there is a freak, almost perpendicular needle-rock called Hayna Picchu, which rises a thousand feet in the air. Next morning we got up in the dark in the little hotel to climb it: it wasn't as bad as it looked; broken Inca steps climbed almost vertically through the tangle of undergrowth; but bad enough. I reached the top with racing pulse in a muck-sweat. A tree-choked ruin is poised on the very top. (We found a red-bearded Scotchman waking up there in his sleeping-bag, which gave us all a bit of a jar.) The place hung there like a magic carpet. The first sunbeams were pouring through clefts in newly revealed ranges of the Andes. They flashed on the faraway glaciers of the Veronica massif and stressed the walls and the tiers below with shadow. Andrew, full of misgivings, had abstained from our early climb, bent on a solitary trial later. He returned in an hour or two and slumped on his bed saying, with sad stoicism: 'Well, it's not for me, I'm afraid.' He's anxious about holding others back, as I am, but I bet he needn't worry.

★   ★   ★

13

We were the only gringos in the carriage on the way back. It was crammed with Quechuas and overflowing with bundles and chickens and papooses. Kind Carl nursed a small Indian boy on his lap. Andrew leaped up, whipped off his linen hat and gave his seat to a bowlered squaw. She sat down without a word or a glance. We took it in turns to relieve him on the jolting platform at the end of the carriage all the way to Cuzco. When we arrived, both the woman and Carl's boy's father disappeared without so much as a *buenos noches*. Many of the Quechua are fine looking, with high-cheeked features of polished bronze, smiles turning down at the corners and hair black and lustrous as a raven's feather.

BACK IN CUZCO   *Later on*

This won't be very coherent.

My room was in chaos an hour ago. Now all is sorted out at last—kitbag, rucksack, ice-pick, those huge waiting boots; zip-bag and attaché case to be left in the care of the Swiss Brewery here with all our other unwanted stuff. The hotel passage is choked with packing-cases containing food and drink for two weeks, fourteen bottles of airport whisky poured into two semi-transparent unbreakable jerrycans, stoves, fuel, cooking pots, coils of rope, lanterns, torches, a communal tent for meals (we each have a small personal one), also lilos, marvellous hooded and padded sleeping-bags, duvets, many layers of pullover and mesh underclothing; and anoraks and cagoules. Andrew, Robin and I have been struggling back from the shops in the Plaza de Armas and the Avenida del Sol again and again all the afternoon under sacks full of pots and pans. We hunted all through the Indian market for a wooden ladle ... It's been rather fun but hard work, of which Robin and Renée have borne most of the brunt, buying the stores and sorting them into packing-cases so that only one of them needs to be opened at a time; a task made no easier by Renée being stricken down for two days by some height-induced illness. The Swiss manager of the brewery here, Mr Mehder and his wife, for whom Carl had an introduction, have been guardian angels with advice, transport, help with the governors and local authorities and the engagement of pack-drivers and ponies. Life is made much easier by André's appointment as treasurer and paymaster-cashier for all expenses. We all cough up when the cash runs low, and he administers it. An arduous task for him, but a marvellous relief for the rest of us.

*   *   *

We plan to follow the Urubamba river once more to the village of Chilca, beyond Ullantaytambo; here we strike up a valley rising from the south bank into a range called Salkantay. When we reach the snow-line, it looks as though Andrew and I will remain at the base camp while the rest of the party conquer the peaks above. It's a bit frustrating; our ignorance would be a hindrance and a danger. But never mind.

Last night when the week's toil was almost complete—the collation of maps, the interviewing of local mountaineers, the negotiations with the Governor and Robin's and Carl's arrangements with the local sub-prefects and *alcaldes* about transport and the assembling of stores—a hitch occurred. A Don Jaime ——, to whom friends in Lima had telephoned asking him to take care of us, was waiting in the hall of the

Conquistador. It was madness, he told us, to go into the Salkantay mountains. With rolling eyes, glances over the shoulder, fingers on lips and stage whispers, he told us that the mountains were full of Communist bandits who would take us prisoner, keep us up in the mountains, and hold us to ransom. (A cutting about our expedition, in *El Comercio*, the Cuzco daily—*Europeos atacarán al Salkantay*—would have tipped them off ...) It happened to some Americans last year, he said. *Look at the Tupamaros!* (There is, it seems, considerable anti-US feeling in Latin America; no anti-British at the moment, thank heavens.) None of the local mountaineers or authorities had murmured a word about all this to us; we concluded that it was a fancy of Don J's. He belongs to the ex-oligarchy who have been expropriated by the present left-wing military regime (whose measures, designed to forestall a Communist takeover, are hotly discussed), and he sees Communists everywhere. For our own good, he was bent on exhorting the Governor to prevent the catastrophe of our adventuring into the mountains unescorted. The Governor, he said, though a nominee of the regime, was *quelqu'un de bonne famille* to whom he could speak frankly ...

Our hearts sank. Robin and I took him out to dinner. The restaurant Roma, in the Plaza de Armas, was full of hippies in ponchos. When two men sat down at the next table, Don J's eyes rolled ominously: '*Chut! Prenez garde! Police secrète! Ils sont partout!*' His stage whisper was overheard by our two neighbours, who were perfectly ordinary American tourists. ('Did you hear that, Tom? Secret police! What the hell!') On parting he left us to wake the Governor up ... We were in despair at the prospect of an infantry battalion escorting us: should we slip away there and then? This morning, however,

Don J was waiting in the hall, all smiles and expansive gestures: 'All's well!' he said. 'You've nothing to worry about! All the villages will be warned—*but not the mayors!* Don't mention it to them!—The secret police will be watching over you wherever you go!—It's all organized! They'll be in the canyons! on the mountains! *partout! Mais vous ne verrez rien! La police secrète est merveilleuse!*' We exchanged glances of wonderment and relief, thinking the whole thing must be a chimaerical fancy of Don J's, kindly meant: the episode is a mixture of Graham Greene and Evelyn Waugh. Or, as André remarked, *Tintin au Temple du Soleil.*[1]

We are taking him out to dinner tonight on our farewell feast. Also the Mehders, our Swiss benefactors from the Cervezeria Cuzqueña. This means jumping conversationally from French to German the whole time. We become fluent and polyglot after a few *pisco* sours and several bottles of wine. (*Pisco* is the local *raki*, very strong and not bad at all.) Robin and I do most of the Spanish interpreting. We are both roughly the same, viz., very limited but voluble. They say Peruvian Spanish is the best in Latin America. There is no Andalusian erosion of consonants, and though Spanish is always referred to as *Castillano*, no Hapsburg lisping of the c's and z's. I wonder if it's the speech of Estremadura, where most of the conquerors were born?

So André is cashier and Andrew has been vaguely appointed botanist to the expedition, in charge of cuttings and seeds. I'm trying to master a few words of Quechua, in case we need it in the mountains. I've not got very far, in spite of a grammar,

[1] Our patronizing attitude was premature, as the present situation in Peru proves clearly enough, and Don J's fears were far from chimaerical.

a dictionary and a book of Quechua poems with Spanish translations and not very expert English ones, e.g.:

In Quechua:

'*Pipa ususinta Kapuwashanki, qan kapuli nawi yunka*
                            sisi hina wiqauchayoi?
Ima urpip takiutaj campa takiykiwan ninakun?'

This means:

'Whose are you daughter, in your capulin eyes and your
                            waist of a jungle ant?
What birdie can to mate your sweet singing?'[1]

Far from plain sailing.

Books. Renée's taking *Illusions Perdues*—how maddening that I read it last year; should we be stuck in camp because of the weather, there'll be a lot of swapping and Balzac is hard to re-read; Robin's got *The Bostonians*, Andrew, *The Spoils of Poynton*, André, *Crome Yellow* and *Antic Hay*, and Carl is deep in my *Oliver Twist*. I'm doing some late prep on Prescott's *Conquest of Peru*, with *Nicholas Nickleby* and *Kim* up my sleeve.

Expectation hangs in the air.

---

[1] In Spanish:

'*Cuya hija eres tu, con esos ojos de capuli y*
    cintura de hormiga tropical?
Que avecilla puede igualar tu dolce canto?'

What indeed? ...

Second Letter

Second Letter

*August 9, 1971   Somewhere above Moyoc-Moyoc in the Sal-
kantay-Huanay range, South-Central Peru. (We're not clear
exactly where we are because all maps conflict. No one except
herdsmen ever seem to have been up here.)*

I SEE I'll have to go over to pencil as the height has affected
the ink in my pen just as it affects everything else. I hope
my eve-of-departure letter arrived all right—it seems that the
stone *bocca di leone* in the wall of the Cuzco post office is only
for *inland* mail. But it should turn up in the fullness of time
... Anyway, I'll charge ahead in my rough and ready style.

We set off on August 5 from the dusty hamlet of Chilca[1]
on the Urubamba river (which, rather confusingly, is also
called the Rio Vilcanota for some of its length) at about noon.
Robin and Andrew had come on earlier with our truck-load
of gear. A kind Milanese *haciendado* (who hasn't been home
for forty years), with a pretty Peruvian wife, helped us and
our two Indian pack-drivers with the unloading, sorting and
reloading of the stuff. At last it was all rather inexpertly lashed
to eight sturdy little ponies. One of these is a near-palomino,
another is a mare with a pretty little four-month-old foal
which trots beside her with minute red-white-red Peruvian
flags threaded through the tips of its ears. The sight of six
gringos, and the gear tumbling off again as soon as it was
loaded, was a godsend to all the watching Indian children and

[1] 8,537 feet above sea-level

21

the dogs of Chilca. Our procession moved off with much waving and shrieking and barking.

We crossed the Urubamba on a plank-floored bridge. Then the path ran beside the river's bank downstream and climbed up and down the mountainside for about three hours. Enough for the first day, we thought, after so late a start. We stopped in a little clearing called Pampa Urubamba,[1] at the entrance to a deep ravine. There were pepper trees and scrub, and organ-cactus and tall leaning blade-like boulders. The river roared below. The two pack-drivers unloaded our eight steeds. They speak to each other in Quechua and to us in Spanish, and their names are Alejandro and Antemio. They are really *ebenístas*—cabinet-makers—by trade. They are the owners of the ponies, and they hire them to us for almost nothing with their services included. They looked a bit unpromising at first but we love them now. (We've had to lend them stockings and jerseys, of which there are mercifully plenty, and we keep them in food. This was not their fault, but the result of bad briefing by the *alcalde* of Chilca.) Both wear thin, ragged town clothes and disintegrating sandals, one has an Afrika Korps cap, the other a battered Anthony Eden. They have rather good, light copper-coloured features, fine high-bridged noses and nice, slightly sad smiles. It was nearly dark by the time everything we needed was unpacked. Renée cooked a delicious stew on a fire of branches and dead trees under one of the vast blades of rock. 'Ah,' she said, when we all extolled it. 'It's only the beginning.'

It was a beautiful night with millions of stars, so we slept

---

[1] I'm not sure this is really its name; any field or flat grassy place is called a pampa.

dotted about the trees. Lulled with two large double whiskies apiece—this is to be our nightly ration for the trip—we were all in our sleeping bags by 8.30, very tired and happy. It seemed just like midnight. How quickly one's time-scheme adapts itself!

Next day, August 6, we got up at 5.30. After breakfast we lolled about talking, while the ponies were being loaded, and moved off at about 9.

We turned inland from the Urubamba, and followed a climbing valley with a stream rushing along the bottom. The canyon was riddled with caves, and now and then we came on a neolithic Indian hamlet among the woods. They were empty of all but a bowler- or top-hatted squaw or two squatting among cows and poultry, in yards that contained a log trough, a stone quern, maize husks, woolly dogs and dust. Occasionally a Quechua in a poncho rode past, his thick criss-cross sandals inserted in square bucket-stirrups of tin. We raise our hats ceremoniously, and 'Salud, señores' comes punctiliously back with an answering flourish. When we greet the squaws, they lift their bowlers as gravely as Guards officers in plain clothes acknowledging a butt-salute; uncovering, as they do so, blue-black hair that is parted in the middle and twisted into two plaits which join a thicker one at the nape of the neck and then hang down their backs interwoven with bright ribbons. (They also take them off in church.) The day was a long switchback of dusty tracks and deep, overgrown and boulder-strewn clefts; but most of the time we were climbing.

We munched chocolate and almonds overlooking a river spanned by a swinging bridge of liana and plank, across which a squealing black pig was being noisily dragged backwards by one leg in the direction of a tumbledown village the other side. A nice old non-Spanish-speaking Quechua—I think the *alcalde*—brought us a jar of *chicha*; white fermented stuff that didn't taste very nice. Exhausted at last at the end of a long and steadily ascending afternoon's trudge, we camped in a glade in the forest, opposite a small sloping pampa where our unloaded ponies were hobbled for grazing above a rushing rocky green stream shaded by leaves. The branches were looped with creepers where humming-birds hovered and lunged like miniature duellists. A little below us, smoke rose perpendicular from the thatched roofs of an Indian village and, the other side of the stream, some Inca ruins guarded a pass that climbed into the bare mountains opposite. Steep and rocky slopes loomed all round. We slept under the stars again, picking out the Southern Cross and, far away to the north, Orion's Belt and the Pleiades. (So *this* is where they go, when we lose them in the summer!) We've been lamenting the lack of a star atlas. There are so many of them, and so bright.

I think this place is called *Aripata*, but I'm not sure. The altimeter showed 9,275 feet. Every now and then, Robin, Carl and André gather and compare the readings on the altimeters that hang round their necks like insignia of the Golden Fleece.

August 7

We toiled all the morning up the flank of a steep and shady canyon while the vegetation changed and grew steadily scarcer. We thought we had lost our baggage-train in the hills, but finally with relief we spied the ponies and the peons, far below and tiny with distance, among the boulders of a river bed. Down we had to go, losing hard-won height. We regained it laboriously, up giant staircases of rock and water and sedgy marshland. The only human beings we met all day were three Indians by a sheepfold. One of them carried a wooden plough and his cheek was bulging with a cud of coca-leaf. They were very friendly but understood not a word of Spanish; not even '¿Donde estan los caballos?'

At last we reached a bleak windy tableland with a few cattle grazing and some yellow-green birds that flew like woodpeckers and a few blue-grey finches. We munched our chocolate and raisins in the lee of a rock, feeling inexpressibly tired: we had climbed a long way fast. The atmosphere and the landscape were both on the move: a chain of ascending glens led us on to a swampy plateau crossed by the scattered slabs of an old Inca road, the far side of which dropped without warning into a wide and grass-floored cauldron. A wall of wavy, spiked rock clambered into the air on all sides; and the taller, snow-topped mountains beyond were wrinkled with glaciers. Two waterfalls were plunging down this palisade and their long arcs, when they struck the cliffs, linked and split and united again until they reached the wide bottom of the cauldron, where fifty loose ponies were grazing among the streams. Large birds, with spectacular white stripes across their black wings, were circling above this gulf and a few vultures hovered. Mist, and then clouds, began blowing down through the gaps in the mountains.

We lay and gazed in wonder and exhaustion; then we heaved ourselves to our feet, which had begun to drag like cannon-balls, and continued the zigzag uphill. We were much higher than we had been in Cuzco now, and, as we plodded on and up, panting like hounds, no second wind came to the rescue. Renée had the idea of swallowing some lemon-flavoured Dextrosol—glucose tablets, that is, which are supposed to get into the bloodstream at lightning speed and attach wings to one's heels. We crammed them down our throats, but still felt like deep-sea divers doing a stretch on a submarine treadmill. The cauldron dropped out of sight and we found ourselves shambling like drunkards along a bare, grassy, whale-backed ridge that rose between two brooks. A moss-covered ruin appeared, and we reeled through the broken wall and collapsed: first Carl, then Andrew, then me. (Andrew and I were neck and neck at the last bit. He murmured 'Not bad for the amateurs!') He doesn't seem to feel the effects of the atmosphere anything like as much as I do, perhaps through non-smoking or some other private dispensation. How groundless his earlier misgivings were! (Tell Debo, as she was anxious, as you were for me. This last bit of keeping-to-the-fore was sheer 'smoker's grit' on my part, I may say. But downhill I'm a human chamois.) The beginners are determined to keep well forward and remain in the first three, in a touching attempt to make a good impression and be allowed a minor share later on. Only Carl is quite impervious to all these rigours—lucky child of the Engadine!—and he has lots of energy left for kindness to the less expert. Robin, Renée and André are free of our erratic variations, and, hounds of heaven, climb and descend with a steady and unwearying pace learnt on many an Alp and Dolomite and Pyrenee. I've never felt so exhausted, though in Greece I've climbed greater distances and for much longer; but never at such heights. Thank heavens, Robin, Renée and André were slightly smitten as well. We set off that morning at 9,273 feet and ended at 13,140, all in seven hours; that is, nearly 4,000 feet. We are more than 2,000 feet above Cuzco now: a lot at these altitudes in so short a time.

The ruined enclosure was an old staging-post on the Inca highway. The walls, pierced by giveaway trapezoidal windows, were six feet high in places and tufted with bushes and trees. They stand at the foot of an enormous purple mountain striped and tiered with strata that make it resemble a vast, overblown Ankor temple. The only other soul in sight was an Indian woman on the slope opposite; she was running as fast as she could, driving a huge flock of sheep downhill over the edge and out of sight; a moment later, an icy wind and a cloud of mist blew down from the temple-mountain. Casting off our torpor with groans, we unpacked all the tents and pitched them, except for two. (For the first time, Andrew and I both slept in the slightly larger mess-tent, to avoid the fag of pitching our smaller ones.) We finished just in time, as it clouded over completely and blew still harder. But we all cheered up when we were huddled on the grass in the big mess-tent. Heroic Renée cooked a comforting stew and Robin sloshed out large whiskies. We were woken up once or twice in the night by the wind and then by the ponies, which were hobbled and coralled in the ruin. They stamped about, occasionally stumbling in the guy-ropes. Then once more to sleep; to sleep, perchance to snore.

MOYOC-MOYOC   *August 8*

When we peered out next morning, the mountains, the ruin, and even the ponies, were white with snowflakes and thick clouds hung low overhead; so everyone rolled over and went to sleep again. We spent most of the day on our backs, acclimatizing hard, as the slightest exertion still left us gasping.

This weather really is bad luck, and it seems without precedent in the Andes at this season. Grey clouds rolled along before driving winds followed by thunder. There's not a word of complaint from Alejandro and Antemio, however, in spite of their thin clothes and sandals, disadvantages which we have tried to remedy. We had borrowed a bivouac for them from the Peruvian garrison in Cuzco, and they cunningly barricaded it in with the packing-cases. They looked very snug inside it, rugged up in ponchos with a fire going and a smoking billy-can. Everything brightens at meal times, when Renée's steaming stews appear, full of onions, garlic and basil; tea spiked with whisky goes down six red lanes. This evening we talked about famous jewellery frauds (Carl), racing scandals (Andrew), French and English books and Caravaggio (apropos of the light and shadow cast by the hurricane lamps in the tent, I think). Jokes ramify and snowball as our journey progresses. It's delightful. We are somewhere above a place called Moyoc-Moyoc—at least, Robin supposes we are—all the maps conflict. I can't resist asking him where we are every so often; back comes the answer: 'M-moyoc M-moyoc',[1] like an awaited couple of bars in a phrase of music.

DEER-TARN   *August 9*

There was blue sky among the clouds this morning so we struck camp, loaded the ponies and set off.

The wild country kept rising and our track circled round the base of the giant red Ankor mountain. Now it's behind us, the last bastion guarding the entrance to a long amphi-

[1] Robin had a slight and rather attractive stammer.

theatre—or stadium, rather—of completely new mountains.

We are in camp at the far end of a slanting prairie of moss and sedge, and the peaks enclosing it are separated by landslides of purple shale and scree. A couple of tarns lower down are the homes of two large black-and-white geese. They flapped away when we broke into their privacy and they have been flying round rather querulously ever since. Apart from some patches of sphagnum, the only vegetation grows in two kinds of green tuft-like balls of wool, but neither shrub nor tree to make a fire. We climbed up three of the ledges at the far end of this prairie before settling—rather unwisely, as it turns out: the soft red shale underfoot has become a chocolate-coloured mud which sticks to everything; we look a horrible mess. The edge of a cliff-like glacier starts half a mile further uphill, and steps up in folds and ridges to a smooth sloping skyline, curling at either end round the bases of two peaks. A desolate, awe-inspiring and rather exciting place.

Clouds gathered fast while we pitched the tents. Then it began to hail, and the hailstones collected in heavy drifts in the folds of the canvas as fast as we stretched it out for pegging. When the tents were up, we crouched in our various shelters till night fell and tea, food and whisky came to the rescue. We crept into our sleeping-bags at half past eight. Some partridge-like birds joined the black-and-white geese, and wheeled about in the darkness with mournful cries.

The height of this camp is 14,663 feet. It's a little lower than the top of Mont Blanc, and very cold.

GOOSE TARN *August 10*

I slept in the mess-tent again. It's much roomier than the claustrophobic bivouacs into which all the others slither at bedtime like contortionists. The privilege involves responsibilities: e.g. this morning, woken by an alarm-clock at five, I put on the Primus and the kettle to brew tea for Robin, Renée and Carl, who were off to reconnoitre the glacier and see what peaks might be attacked. It was a cold, dark dawning with low clouds. As it got light I watched them trudge uphill to the rim of the glacier. Here they roped up and strapped on their crampons. By now, André and Andrew had joined me and we followed them through binoculars as they slowly zigzagged up the cliffs and the folds of the glacier, Carl leading the way and chopping steps with his ice-axe: we could hear it going tok! tok! tok! Then up they went as slowly as flies and vanished into a white fold, to appear much later on the skyline; soon to disappear again. At this moment a huge pale bird with a prodigious wingspan floated out of the battlements of the peak and hovered overhead. '¿Que pájaro es esto?' we cried. '¡El Condor!' the peons answered. The Condor! A wonderful moment! The vast creature swooped and hovered several times during the day, or floated like a spy.

My writing is erratic because I'm in a sleeping-bag and a puffy blue duvet; one hand is gloved, the other filthy from decarbonizing the Primus; my fingers get crusted with muck that no brush, soap or alcohol can move—only this paper, as you see. I'm Lord of the Primus; ah, the pricking and pumping and overflowing and blazing up! A kettle at this altitude takes one and a half hours to boil; at least, ours does. By the way, we all carefully observed in Cuzco and Lima that water *does* flow out of the basin anti-clockwise south of the Equator. We wondered whether port does the same after dinner and if waltzes start in reverse. Everything was frozen solid this morning, and unfolding my towel was like straightening out bent tin.

Just after the condor's visit, the peons started pointing up the mountainside, crying '¡Venado!' and there, three-quarters of the way up a landslide, a very large deer was moving upwards at a slant and starting a succession of minor landslides of its own; a stag with its antlers moulted for the winter, I think. The peons at once shot up a parallel slope as fast as Speedy Gonzales, the Quickest Mouse in Mexico. They hoped to outflank it—as they explained later—then hobble it with an improvised bolas made of girth-rope and stones, and finally dispatch it with a knife. In two hours they were back, smiling but empty-handed. Andrew washes the plates and I do the drying. We've become extremely brisk, and André, toiling at some other chore, compares the technique to Laurel and Hardy.

The climbers came back in the late morning. They hadn't been able to see much from the top of the glacier owing to an untimely onrush of cloud and blown snow. But they found themselves unexpectedly close to one of the three summits of Huanay: they tackled it. But they were soon waist-deep in new powder snow; so they have had to chuck it until a crust forms for them to cut steps. They were a bit depressed about this unpropitious weather—especially Renée, usually so stoical.

The awfulness of our muddy and sodden camp-site suddenly dawned on us. We tore down the tents, flung them on the ponies and, stooping under surplus gear, rushed helter-skelter down to the little moss-covered prairie below and pitched camp again. Only just in time, as hail came bouncing down, and then snow. It turned into a real blizzard, accompanied by lightning and a thunderstorm. Soon everything outside was white. Safe in the mess-tent the beginners listened wide-eyed to tales of thunderstorms in the high *arêtes* where the electricity makes one's hair stand literally on end and the ice-axe hisses in one's grasp like a snake ...

The tents were now embedded in several inches of snow. The lamplight, glowing through the canvas in this white hushed landscape, looks very pretty after dark. My new home measures ten feet by seven and it is six feet high. The roof, sagging with the weight of the snow, drips a bit through holes that we plan to repair with adhesive tape and every so often we beat the snow off. Inside, we are mattressed with sleeping-bags, and there are carefully arranged lilos and kitbags to lean on. When all faces are lit from below by lanterns and candles, our lair has enormous charm. Its incumbents form a rather Peacockian assembly: an ex-ski champion jeweller, a lawyer-cum-anthropologist, a landowner-race-horse owner; two writers, Robin and me—this puts it off balance a bit—and one—but one can't possibly call Renée a housewife. Her role tonight, ladling out steaming ravioli which we washed down with hot toddy, is more that of a quiet-voiced Wendy ministering to five Lost Boys of riper years in an Andean Never-Never-Land. The drink—two generous doubles apiece (and more on special nights like this)—is lasting well. Conversation is varied, far-ranging, funny and refreshingly indiscreet. Laughter rings across the snow. I wonder what Alejandro and Antemio make of it all, huddling in their little nook a few yards away.

To wash and shave, we crawl out to frozen streams. André, Carl and Andrew set a very good example. One feels reborn after these lustral sessions. Robin has given up shaving in the mountains, and, like me, sleeps fully clothed except for his boots; the others struggle into Charvet pyjamas before wriggling Houdini-like into their cocoons. Thanks to ash and the muck of the Primus, I look a hopeless tramp; but Robin, unfairly, appears steadily more distinguished as the days pass (*Il s'habille avec un chiffon*, like Lilia Ralli) except that those blond bristles bestow a very slightly raffish Evangelical look, giving just a touch of the dissolute sheriff. Renée manages to stay clean, tidy, trim and sibylline; Pythian among the fumes ... The sun has turned Andrew's face into an ebullient tomato still deeper in hue than his pullover. 'Far be it from me ...' is a frequent conversational opening of his and 'I don't want to strike a discordant note ...'—preludes to high-speed and very funny anecdotes. He has a fleetingly wistful look on days when a horse is running. He and André have to double up their long legs in the narrow mess-tent, knees to chin. André, at the end of a sentence, peers with raised eyebrows and an interrogatory smile at his closest neighbour with an almost voiceless 'Hm?', inviting confirmation. Carl's unfailing expression of wonder is a charming and rather old-fashioned 'Go on?'

The padded duvets expand our torsos and arms to the bulk of Renaissance doublets. Except for Carl's, which is a workmanlike beige, they are staring blue or scarlet—to make one, I suppose, easily discernible at a distance in case of mishap. Robin and Renée have proper mountaineering breeches; these, and our corduroy trousers, are tucked into cheerful red or green stockings, though the Feddens sometimes wear some very recherché black ones. Carl has ingenious trousers invented by himself, which buckle on his boots to keep the snow out, like cavalry overalls. Up here, where it is so cold, we wear brightly coloured Balaclava helmets, except for Robin and Renée, who have those conical woollen caps with a bobble, like Calabrian bandits. At lower altitudes, everyone wears a white linen hat against the sun, except me, that is. My thin Cuzco sombrero has a battered *Death in Venice* look, from being stowed in my rucksack. This film comes a lot into our conversation, as we have all just seen it.

GOOSE TARN   *August 11*

A great day for the beginners! It was a brilliant and cloudless morning. Except for Renée, who was to hold the fort, we all set off up the ledges to the glacier's foot. Here we lashed on our crampons; Andrew's and mine only cover our insteps, unlike the great long-toothed harrows, stretching the entire length of their boot-soles, which the others wear. Then we smothered our faces with Swedish anti-sun grease and special anti-lip-cracking paste that made us all look like Al Jolson. We put on dark goggles, pulled down our hats; then Carl was roped to Andrew, and I between Robin and André. We got on the glacier by chopping steps with our axes—or rather, by treading where the ice lay already dinted by Carl. Soon we were on a crust of snow-covered ice curving like a giant meringue. Climbing a few yards apart, we next went up some minor slanting cliffs; again with steps we had cut in the ice. We bestrode several narrow but very deep crevasses that curved clean across the crisp mounting surface. You have to keep banging your boots with the ice-axe, as snow packs solid

34

between the teeth of the crampons and turns them into heavy weights that can become slippery as skates. It was an undulating, brilliantly sparkling wilderness. Breathing was still short of normal; but I really had the feeling of being acclimatized at last. The ascent was steep and laborious but unhurried; considerate Robin, who was leading my little group, made frequent halts which were very welcome to André as well as to me: the aftermath of an old pleurisy conspired with the altitude to act as a brake when he least wished it.

I can't exaggerate the beauty of the empty whiteness stretching from height to height, or the brilliance of the snow in the sun, or the elliptical, magnesium-blue loops of shadow. The glitter of a frozen waterfall broke through the snow wherever the glacier took an abrupt upward tilt; and, under sudden juts of snow, horizontal clefts, barred with flashing icicles, opened like whales yawning. The crevasses, over which we stepped so lightheartedly, plunged to great depths. The blue-green transparency deepened until the light, which was only faintly dimmed by the crust of snow on either side of these clefts, at last died away in shadow far below. To lift one's dark glasses for a moment was to touch off an explosion of dazzle ... After two hours of climbing and halts, we reached our goal. It was the windy col that formed the skyline from our camp, which now seemed as far below as the bottom of the Pacific. We followed Carl's and Andrew's footprints over the saddle, and slid down to the snowless ledge where they were lying on the dry shale on the other side. We pulled off our anoraks and sweaters and sprawled beside them, all our cramponed boots dangling in the blazing sunlight. We were just over 15,000 feet up. It was a moment of great euphoria, and, for us, near-intoxication: after all our misgivings, we'd actually *crossed a glacier, roped up, shod with crampons and wielding ice-picks, 600 feet above the summit of Mont Blanc!* The old hands, for whom this was a common routine, rejoiced for our sake.

Our ledge was on a level with an infinity of peaks retreating to an enormous distance. From one side to the other of some of these great chasms, the lower world was closed over by a lid of thin cloud, or of precariously balanced planes of separate, loosely dovetailing puffs. These cohered as they retreated in rippling threadbare veils of vapour, sometimes transparent and sometimes opaque, and forming an intermittent sea. The mountain salients became headlands or outlying islands and the re-entrants were bays and inlets—you almost expected to see harbours hovering there. Along the valleys that were free of this illusory sea our glance could travel unhindered for leagues. We could gaze down to the bottom of canyons where the mineral, rising from a ruffle of vegetation and the hint of streams, soared in walls of mountain where the continuous faults and ledges answered each other from massif to massif like the retreat of an echo. The peaks sprang up in leaning table mountains and triangles streaked with black and por-phyry; some of them looked as soft to the touch—and the same colour—as wallflower-petals. These lesser peaks were overtopped by white heights like our own; the glaciers were wrinkled and pleated between their shining crests; and the corridors winding away beyond them always ended in a final sierra of uninterrupted white; or, depending on the position of the sun, in a blue serration almost as thin and pale as the sky.

Only immediately to the east of our vantage point were these vistas shut out: the white saddle where we were sitting dipped a little and then continued its eastward ascent, gently at first, then more steeply, until it ended in a tall round peak: the first of the three summits of Huanay. Linked by cols, they go leap-frogging away into the void. The state of the snow had foiled yesterday's attack, but Robin and Carl were bent on a second try and we watched their silhouettes grow smaller over the bright snow until they disappeared. They returned in two hours having climbed some of the way up the peak, but they were soon knee-deep in fresh powder snow, then up to their waists. Far too dangerous to continue. There was nothing for it but to wait and pray that the weather changes enough for a crust to form.

At last we roped up again for the descent. They say this is even more important on the way down; especially for the one in front. Sometimes he has to advance on all fours to peer over the rim of a ledge, while his companions stand back to support him in case there is a brittle overhang. I had never understood the roping principle, thinking that the fall of one climber would bring the others hurtling down too, like a row of skittles; but I've got the point now. I was following Robin along the flank of a slope, and, emboldened by success, much too fast. Suddenly my foothold went; I fell a few feet; then began to skid down a milder incline of glacier—only to be pulled up suddenly about three yards along it, thanks to Robin and André both leaning back to take the strain. It wasn't a very forbidding slope, or I wouldn't have risked such a pace, nor a very alarming event; but I might have gone skiddering down for a hundred yards or so, where I think the slope ended in soft snow. Carl charitably blamed it on our beastly crampons: some of the short teeth of mine were bent inwards when I took them off, giving no purchase at all. One needs those great steel lobsters the others clank about in.

The sun went in behind low hanging clouds, making the snowscape rather eerie and also rather magnificent in a melancholy way; those blue-green caves stalactitic and stalagmitic with icicles were now faintly sinister. We got down to the shale and the moss at last, where we unroped and decramponed in the mud of the melting glacier; then down, past our old camp at Deer Tarn; and lower still to Goose Tarn, where we are now. The geese rose as we approached, and flew in a ring overhead. Carl looked round the bleak scene, and said: 'No sign of Don J's secret police!' and of kidnapping bandits, *tampoco*. Alerted by our cries of triumph Renée was waiting outside the mess-tent in her blue duvet. It seemed as if we had been away for a month.

We fell asleep and were awoken by the cry of those geese just as a sulphurous sun was setting through the beginnings of a snowfall. The geese are getting much tamer; in a month they would be snuggling beside us. Alejandro and Antemio are tucked up in their cunningly barricaded bivouac, and our eight ponies—nine including the foal—are dotted about in the gloaming, all spectral with snow. It's colder than ever and the water is frozen solid in the canvas buckets. But the Primus in the mess-tent hisses dutifully under the kettle, the lanterns are lit, and I can hear the others coming across like five Captains Oates. All prospects glow.

Perhaps not for all, but for the beginners it's a day to be marked with a white stone. It can't *not* have happened, now. These are Late Developers' Joys.

STILL AT GOOSE TARN   **August 12**

It's colder than ever. I woke at 5 a.m., long before dawn, and put on the Primus for Robin, Renée and Carl. They decided last night to go up again and assault the three summits of Huanay. With icy fingers they accoutred themselves with gaiters, ropes, torches, ice-axes, duvets, gauntlets and Bala-clavas and then moved off across the white plateau while dawn was breaking. The rest of us huddled shivering all day over our books and letters, until at last, in the afternoon, we descried our three comrades descending the glacier. In an hour they were within hailing distance; when they came lower, we could tell by their jubilant signals that all had gone well. Tremendous embraces and high spirits broke out when they reached the base. Everything had been perfect—*all three summits climbed*! I'm so glad. Robin was getting more and more concerned about the weather putting a stop to things— a seven-thousand-mile journey, all in vain! The three peaks are connected by saddles and the highest is just under 15,000 feet. As they reached the top of the last peak, a huge condor sailed out of the side of the mountain below them, and glided away into the void.

I read some of *The Conquest of Peru* out loud after dinner. We were all very much taken by Prescott's closing words about the llama: 'It is only when overloaded that the spirited little animal refuses to stir, and neither blows nor caresses can induce him to rise from the ground'—exactly like us, we all thought. By the end of the chapter, all heads had drooped and all eyelids closed. It might have been a cradle song ... a gentle harmony of snores.

TWO RIVERS   *August 13*

Everybody—we, *los peones* and the ponies—were delighted
to leave this rather bleak and forbidding place. It was palisaded
all round by cataracts of shale and the clouds rolled over it
like a gas attack. (It had a desolate charm, nevertheless.) All
were pleased, that is, except the geese, who followed us on
foot at first, and when we reached the pass (marked by a cairn
of rocks on the old Inca road, to which we each added a
stone) they rose up and wheeled above our heads lamenting.
Or so we interpreted it.

We headed east. All day long we threaded a path down
the right flank of a deep and tortuous ravine. Valleys came
down to join it from the southern peaks, and rushing streams,
collecting in blue-green pools banked with moss and grass,
overflowed in waterfalls. A succession of slanting sunbeams
spanned the canyon. Sometimes the ponies were below us;
more often we left them behind. Sprawling beside these
beautiful pools, we watched them twisting down the steep
corkscrew path, with the peons' exhortations echoing downhill. They were always the same: '*¡Caramba!*', which Robin
and I took to be an old-fashioned equivalent of 'Great
Heavens!' In sterner moments, they more dashingly cried
'*¡Ca-rájo!*' through bared teeth. When they caught up,
Alejandro and Antemio would sit with us for a smoke while
the ponies drank. The foal still wears its little ear-flags.

A perpendicular massif formed the left wall of this canyon
and climbed to spikes of sunlit snow far overhead. Stripes of
blue, rust, saffron, orange, mauve and purple mottled and
streaked the precipices, and at the bottom of the ravine
tumbled a growing torrent. As we lost height, those half-

woodpecker, half-cormorant-looking birds reappeared again among the low trees. There were downy yellow cactuses with butter-coloured flowers, and yuccas opening sharp corollas of blades on every ledge. Their roots split the rocks overhead and tufted the cliffs opposite with green constellations. We scanned every ledge for deer and the air for condors but we only spotted a vulture or two and some more of those black-and-white hovering birds. Through field-glasses, beside a lake in a sudden widening plunge of the canyon, we picked out a drinking pony; it was the first sign of contemporary human beings for many days, as the regions we were abandoning were totally uninhabited and largely unnamed. They must be some of the least known and remotest parts of the Andes. The peons were very excited, as this and all the last week's terrain was *terra ignota* to them as well as us.

Towards late afternoon we reached a most beautiful plateau. Grassy slopes enclose it with golden-green shelves, and tall black cliffs beetle, plumed and striated and separated by multi-coloured alluvial cones. Above these, corridors and causeways and staircases of mountain lead up and away into airy stone glades slanting with shafts of sunlight and shadow, all of them culminating in half a dozen beckoning white summits which have already kindled a spark in the eyes of the mountaineers ... A cascade flashes high above the far side of this enclosed oblong, curvetting from hollow to hollow and falling in long, pale jade ostrich-feathers of water. After striking the level, it divides into two serpentine rivers that meander across the little plateau. This is only half a mile long, sparsely littered with geometric fragments of rock the size of hay-ricks. A few islands break up the current of these two streams, and ten ponies and twenty-six cows graze on their banks.

41

There is an exit to the lower world at the other end. A wall of boulders surrounds a stone hovel with a single smoky room and one or two prehistoric utensils, the abode of six dogs and two top-hatted shepherdesses and their papooses. They appeared from the heights just as we were pitching camp, driving a large flock. Sheep, goats, lambs and kids trickled slowly down, filling the hollow with bleating and barking and echoes, casting long evening shadows up the mountainside. The ponies began rolling joyfully the moment they were unsaddled.

Yucca stalks, fallen from the precipice by the thousand, scatter the ledge where our tents are pitched. They look like battered motor-bike cylinders, and burn beautifully, especially when eked out with dried cow-pats. Carl, washing in the waterfall, startled a big marten-like animal, and, much higher up, someone caught a glimpse of a huge hare, the size of a collie dog, it seems; it is called a *viscacha*, I think. We had noticed the tracks of both on the snow and wondered what they were. In the woods lower down, there are pumas; they attack ponies but not humans, so there's hope. We drink *maté de coca* after supper—it is a mild infusion of the coca-leaf. We haven't been able to get any actual coca; though all the peons except ours seem to chew it. Mixed with potash, it keeps them going for ever in a mild trance.

There are amazing stars at night.

August 14

I took one of Andrew's Seconals last night, to get through the long cold hours that Soneril doesn't quite seem to span.

It was a real *comprimé Céline*[1] ... When I woke, everyone was having breakfast round my sleeping-bag. It was rather nice. There was a lot of teasing about Roman Emperors and *Les Rois Fainéants*. Robin: 'G-get the m-marmalade away from V-Volpone, w-will you, Renée?' Why not summon the shepherdesses, indeed, and all their sisters from the plains and finish the journey by palanquin ...?

Robin, Carl and Renée were bent on scaling the peak immediately above. Robin had had his eye on it ever since Huanay, where he spied it in the distance. Andrew and I would have liked to have gone with them, but our diffident suggestions were not taken up, quite rightly: it would have been monkeys playing the violin, only more dangerous. The plan was to get bivouacs and supplies up there on a couple of ponies as far as the glacier line; but it was so steep that the peons, to spare the ponies, preferred to carry all the gear themselves; and so they did—two pony loads of it. (*Question*: Who would fardels bear? *Answer*: Alcjandro and Antemio.) Andrew accompanied them for a couple of hours, then came down, some of the time simply sitting and sliding down steep grass. He strayed for a while, but reached camp in the early afternoon. André stayed behind, declaring, gloomily but not credibly, that his climbing days were over; and I was bent on carrying on with this letter. I idled the day away, wallowing in the peaceful beauty of this plateau, lying on a bank of moss reading Prescott. (Do you remember reading *The Conquest of Mexico*, years ago, lying in hammocks in the Petén jungle in Guatemala?)

The two peons got back, grinning widely and holding up

---

[1] *Voyage au Bout de la Nuit* ...

two enormous ducks that they had, quite amazingly, contrived to kill with stones on an upland lake: black-and-white birds with purple flashes on their wings. They cooked and ate one there and then, keeping the other for us. (But it was a bit sad; the birds had probably never even seen any human beings before, so feared nothing.) When the duck was swallowed, they borrowed the string bag we keep the onions and the garlic in and went down to the stream; half an hour later, they were back with a large trout floundering in the mesh. They are phenomenal. We sent them down the valley to bargain with the shepherdesses for potatoes—Peru is the old pre-Conquest home of potatoes and there are over eighty different kinds. They came back with their ponchos full, and Andrew, André and I roasted some in the embers for supper. Afterwards, I managed to persuade André to tell us the saga of his adventures in the French army and during the fall of France. He escaped from the Germans across the Pyrenees and lay in hiding in Madrid, and finally got to England from Bilbao. This was followed by service in the Free French Air Force, then SOE training in Scotland, after which he was dropped by parachute into the Vosges and worked in the Resistance till the end of the war in Europe. An exciting story, beautifully and amusingly told.

In spite of a sunstroke-fraught blaze all day, the nights are bitter.

August 15

We took turns to wash our handkerchiefs and things in the waterfall. Total immersion followed, under the hurtling tons of cloudy green glacier-water. After this, with small-clothes stretched on the boulders to dry, we lay on the grass, watching the yucca- and dung-smoke ascend into a cloudless sky while the flocks and the cattle climbed to their pastures. Andrew shot energetically up the mountainside, till he was nothing but a pink pullover and white hat high above.

Early in the afternoon, Carl got back, stooping under most of the gear of the camp; and two hours later, Robin and Renée. They all looked very tired. They had found a beautiful place to bivouac just under the glacier-line. It was a reedy plateau with a string of lakes covered with waterfowl, and dropped abruptly to a wonderful disorder of lesser mountains. In the end, Robin and Carl attacked the peak alone. It's the day after now and we have been peering at the peak through binoculars (it is invisible from the camp itself) and we could clearly follow their tracks in the snow almost to the summit. All went well until they began the last steep ascent to the cone. Here the hard snow began to soften and they sank in waist-deep with nothing hard underfoot. The snow then became as loose as sand; there was no purchase at all, and it was ready to slide *en masse*. To have carried on up the steadily steepening slope might probably have pulled an avalanche down on them and carried them two thousand feet into a chasm. So they had to turn back and fumble their way down again to a firm foothold. Better weather conditions, and hard snow in which they could have cut steps, would have carried them to success. But it was a moral victory. They were only twenty yards short of the top! There were delicious boiled potatoes mashed up with butter for dinner, and the second of the peons' ducks, which was rather stringy.

SILQUE PAMPA   *August 16*

We were sorry to leave this beautiful place. It's one of the highest pastures in the world, and the peons say that no strangers have ever been here. The shepherdesses, whom we have watched from our knoll every day as they lead their flocks out and home again, have kept very much to themselves. Out of shyness, perhaps; but none of the Indians we have seen on our journey have asked who we are or where we come from. This is rather a relief, when one thinks of the cross-questioning swarm that a stranger's presence summons by magic out of a bare Turkish landscape—or a Greek one, for that matter. But, bearing in mind that we must seem as strange to them as Martians, there is something a bit puzzling about this incurious apathy, unless it's fear: atavistic reserve implanted by centuries of stratified Inca oligarchy, followed by the shock of the *Conquista*, and then four hundred years of Spanish rule; it must have made all strangers suspect; especially to remote star-dwellers like these. The Indians are very friendly when tackled with due ceremony. They have rather grave good manners.

Our caravan moved off. The plateau was sprinkled with gentians, and among them lay the skeleton of a pony, dismembered and scattered by vultures with flowers and grass springing up through the ribs. Beyond the shepherdesses' cottage were two empty homesteads of boulder and thatch, where the only signs of occupation were the mounds of seed potatoes, a bristly backed boar, and a portentous black sow with her inky farrow of eight. As we emerged through the gateway of two mountains, a V of downland opened up between the craggy sides; and, far away at the end, covered with snow from the bottom to the tip, glittered the huge Fujiyama-Matterhorn apparition of the Veronica. A new world, once more.

The mountains drew back on either side of an airy lift and fall of savannah. As our caravan picked its way over the edge and headed downhill, orange-flowered organ-cactus and myrtle and tamarisk rose up and the air began to smell of spice. There was a blazing sky of very pale blue. All the streams and waterfalls that flowed on to the plateau united near this threshold and took the downhill path under the name of Rio Silque; and when the mule track changed banks, we waded up to our thighs through icy jadeite glacier-water coiling breakneck through the boulders over a bed of moving pebbles; then the path soared up over a shoulder of the left-bank mountains through open downland and savannah. Bit by bit, the jaws of the canyon began to narrow again, forcing us more steeply down. The file of ponies gave a processional gravity to our descent. The vegetation grew taller and thicker, butterflies began to hover, the birds multiplied; then shady branches swallowed us up. The path rocketed up and down under the trees, but when the converging sides of the canyon began to straighten into the vertical and actually to impend, it was all downhill: a twisting ladder of rocks and dust and dead leaves that led us in and out of shade, and, at last, alongside the river itself. Reinforced by a score of streams and still blue-green, except where it was opaque with commotion, the river crashed down a staircase of cataracts, splitting and joining round smooth white boulders and hissing through narrows. When the bed sank in a deep basin, the face of the water was still enough, under the shadow of the heightening trees, to offer a flawed and dappled reflection of

47

the branches. The trees were covered with lichen and strung with lianas; and parasites spread tufts along the branches like the head-dresses of caciques. We were descending one of those chasms of water and leaves on which, a few days ago, we had looked loftily down from the glacier.

It is impossible to say what the trees, the flowers and the birds really were. Each of them *looks* like something familiar, but when you peer closer, it's not it. You would see an apparent ragged robin, then notice that it was growing on a thorny stalk ... Many of the trees resembled mimosas and acacias, and there were larger ones with leaves of dark-green mackintosh that might have been *Magnolia grandiflora* and shrubs with yellow flowers emerging from a ring of falling lanceolate leaves. Others were hung with dried pods or with pods encased in silver felt; there were solitary 'delphiniums' here and there—but I expect they weren't, so I won't go on qualifying—and a kind of passion-flower; walnut trees, *ceiba* and near-mahogany, and, underneath, brambles that might have been raspberries or blackberries all entangled with convolvulus and deadly nightshade. The path descended hour upon hour, sometimes so steeply that it seemed a spiral; overhung with branches at one moment and looking down on tree-tops the next; and as we lost height, variety and density increased. Breadfruit and pawpaws appeared, and mare's-tails, and enormous bamboos and white tufted pampas grass, and high, elaborate umbellifers. The forest resembled one of those watery and melancholically beautiful wild gardens in Cornwall or the west of Ireland; an illusion so compelling that an ivied Gothick ruin would hardly have come amiss.

The ponies manoeuvred their way down this dark path

with difficulty. They floundered badly in one steep and muddy patch where all was rank and rotten and a-squelch with shifting and alligatorish logs. The river fell so sharply sometimes that great fans of spray and spindrift were flung up by the boulders that nearly dammed it. Again and again the pathway changed banks across uncouth Indian suspension bridges hung high over the river, woven of branches and liana and floored with slats on which the earth, now dripping with vegetation, had been laid and beaten flat. They swayed and dipped as we went over them. Not all the ponies would risk it; these had to be taken across at lower fords, bravely breasting the foam half-submerged under their rocking loads. At one ford only the foal's little pennanted head was visible above the flood; it scrambled ashore, eyes wide with reproach. The last of these bridges must have snapped a few years ago; the pendent wreckage disintegrated in the water on either side which was half-blocked by boulders flinging up rainbows of spray. We tied our boots round our necks and plunged across. It was a magical day: one wanted the enchanted descent, sinking mysteriously from zone to zone, never to end.

The jaws of the canyon began to open; the two precipices slanted less steeply back. The Veronica, still blazing at the end of the V, had floated up twice and then three times the height it had looked at the top of the pass. At last an ominous potato patch showed among the trees and the rocks, a yam or cassava bed, a clump of eucalyptus, a stack of enormous adobe bricks, logs hollowed into troughs and a few broken earthenware pots; then, three black cows, obstinately blocking the path, showed that we were back in human regions. It was the edge of a rambling village. Smoke rose from the thatch below and

Indians were ploughing the middle distance with black and piebald bulls. A squaw with a papoose on her back scuttled out of her hut and saluted us in turn—Carl, Andrew, André and me, that is—by removing her bowler and touching each of our arms ceremoniously with it between the elbow and the shoulder. It was a charming, enigmatic gesture. We gave her a bar of chocolate. She looked at it in surprise then murmured something in Quechua, and dashed into her hut, returning with a plate of maize which we nibbled with solemnity. Her thick, many pleated skirt was edged with a wide hem of elaborately tooled leather. Robin and Renée, a quarter of a mile behind, were offered' *chicha* with similar punctilio.

The exit-cliffs to this canyon looked like a melting cathedral on one side and a ruined castle on the other. They funnelled the valley then spread it wide across the outside world. It was evening now and we were very tired, but the foal was tiredest of all. It was beginning to stumble and at last the spirited little animal came to a standstill, like Prescott's llamas when overtaxed. André tried to make it swallow some lemon-flavoured Dextrosol, but it refused, so Antemio slipped his poncho under its belly, lifted it off the ground, slung it over his shoulder and trotted the remaining five miles with the little pony on his back, its head and forelegs hanging out at one end, and hindlegs and tail the other. They both looked quite happy and I think he would have done the same if it had been a grand piano.

Between us and the Veronica flowed the Urubamba river once more. Peasants padded past us in the dust. A ring of Indians carousing in a field waved their bottles in invitation. We were back on the edge of civilization: the path ran past fields and maize plantations and haciendas, and we heard the bell of a train in the distance: the Machu Picchu Special from Cuzco! We were downcast to be leaving those solitary and news-free wildernesses, and there was a touch of that nameless dread in the air that haunts all such returns. (What revolutions, plagues and inter-planetary wars might not have broken out?) This place—Silque Pampa—seemed a tame region after our heights; but we were still 8,556 feet above the sea.

We pitched the mess-tent in a field as night fell, and cheered up on the lashings of whisky still miraculously left over from our rationing in the mountains. It was warm enough to sleep out again. The ponies munched and whinnied all round us for the last time. Alejandro and Antemio, grinning and voluble with *chicha*, rolled happily back from the pueblo at midnight. What were those shapes at the bottom of the field? Goalposts! It was the last straw.

URUBAMBA (8,700 feet)   August 17

There were millions of stars last night, and we woke up under a pale dazzling sky with cumulus clouds drifting above the snow and the ice of the surrounding sierras. The peons brought us a slouch hat full of fresh brown eggs from the Italian's hacienda at Chilca (our starting place: we have come full circle). We boiled them and ate them on the grass, surrounded by yellow clouds of giant broom. Flocks were scattered over the hillside and Indians peered benevolently at us through the huge pewter-coloured leaves of a maguey hedge. We filled our water-bottles and watered the ponies at the fountain at the Hacienda Primavera where the friendly Italian *haciendado*'s Indian wife begged us to come indoors *para tomar un cafe y un*

51

poquito de musica on the gramophone. But it was late morning, so we pressed on down an avenue of tall eucalyptus which, Robin admitted, was a fine stand of timber. It seemed a lifetime ago that we had crossed the Urubamba on the same plank bridge, the day we set out. At the railway-halt at Chilca, scores of blanketed Indians were squatting among the rails. We struck east and upstream along a main road beside the river.

The Urubamba is as wide as the Thames above Oxford here; green and fast and hemmed in with fields and trees. Black-and-white swifts were darting low over the ripples and through the pepper trees and the blue-green eucalyptus. The adobe and thatch villages were strewn with giant clay amphorae and tufted with rose-bushes and enormous weeping willows that swayed in the breeze. Sickles and scythes gleamed where the Indians were mowing in the river-meadows.

Renée and I found ourselves a long way behind the others, and the ponies were a long way behind us. Caked with dust we trudged grimly along the main road under a blazing noon sun. For a few furlongs, we walked along the sizzling railway track, but the sleepers were just too widely set for a walking pace. There were numbers of *chicha* booths, each marked by a red flag, in lieu of an inn-sign. We kept asking how far it was to our goal, and the answer from the Indians, all taking it easy in the shade, was always the same: '*Dos leguas, señores* ...' But at last the two leagues were behind us and we staggered into Ullantaytambo.

We soon saw we were in an extremely odd town. It's more than three-quarters Inca and of the most bold and megalithic type. The streets were filled with Quechuas. Cyclopean walls and staircases sprawled down to the river and climbed the steep mountainside in tiers; huge terraces and fortifications impended. An immense Cyclopean square marked the central plaza and colossal lintels of granite spanned the doors of the houses all round it. Squared blocks of porphyry many tons in weight and slotted for lost sacrificial purposes lay about the place. Lanes of hewn and leaning boulders branched away and streams rushed under rough and massive bridges. Everything is battered, decayed, dust-caked, cactus-choked, teeming, eerie and enigmatic; but so monumental that it can never collapse. There is something disturbing about these huge Hispano-Incaic plazas, doubly so at midday. They were frequent scenes of horror under both regimes: dismemberment, disembowelling, tearing apart by horses, sawing in half, garotting, decapitation and burning. Gasping in the noon heat we found the others drinking beer in a smaller plaza and made a dash for the bottles. All round our rickety chairs squaws were squatting by their baskets and their mounds of humble wares. Blank eyes watched us, snot fossilized in infant nostrils, and stinging dust blew across the stone slabs in whiffs of grapeshot. The farewells with Antemio and Alejandro were sincere and moving: they grasped hands and wrists with both of theirs in turn, and headed back for their village in a sad cloud of dust. The foal was quite itself again. Valedictory emotion ran high on both sides.

In the late afternoon, the most ramshackle truck in Peru, hired for a song and piled high with our stuff and with us, rattled and crept upstream through woods and mountains to the little town of Urubamba itself.

*　　　*　　　*

Ghostly with dust, and probably pretty smelly, we clumped with our huge boots into the shiny and table-reflecting precincts of a smart little government hotel. Waiters in white jackets hung about; the walls of a softly lit bar were hung with the skins of pumas, tigrillos and wild boar. It all seemed very strange indeed, and we were overcome with slightly lunatic hilarity. When we emptied our rucksacks and kitbags in our spacious rooms, out cascaded showers of dirty clothes, stockings, socks, rolls of bumf, twisted candles, melted chocolate, straw, burrs, compasses and raisins covered in fluff. With hair plastered down after showers like children at a choir treat, we sat down to a gracious candlelit dinner in a vaulted alcove. But we discovered that though we drank lots of wine at high speed, we could only eat about a quarter of the many courses. Up in the mountains we had scarcely eaten anything except what Renée had cooked in the evening; and wanted nothing else: one kept going on chocolate and raisins and almonds during the day. In spite of the climbing and the sun, one sweated scarcely at all; but we've all lost weight— my belt's in two notches!—and we all feel miraculously well and buoyantly happy; gorged with marvels to chew on for years. Spirits were never higher than tonight, especially as the empty bottles mounted up. The Quechua waiters looked at each other askance at the noise and the laughter. Fortunately we are the only people in the hotel.

We breakfasted off pawpaws and eggs and bacon under an umbrella on the threadbare lawn next to a kidney-shaped bathing pool. A young Texan couple, whom we had seen yesterday in Ullantaytambo, came and joined us. They had bought a pony for their stuff. He is about twenty-three, she *looked* about fourteen, and is very pretty in a dotty way;

both were in ponchos and sandals and he had steel-rimmed spectacles, a fluttering blond beard and long hair caught in at the nape with a rubber band. They are studying the old Inca roads; they are also, in a rather nebulous fashion, searching for the centre of the Essene sect, which they say is hidden somewhere in South America. They were vague about them; and vaguer still about Yogi, Sufism and Dervishes. They regard all these as American—indeed, Californian—phenomena with possible, forgotten Asiatic associations ... Andrew and Robin decided that they probably found our auras rather earthy. (Over to ink. My pen has suddenly recovered in the reduced height, so I am finishing this letter in style.)

CUZCO   August 18

For a fiver we hired another lorry to take us to Cuzco. We lay comfortably in the back, cushioned among rucksacks and kitbags under a few fast clouds. The river, roofs, towers and trees of Urubamba were soon behind us, also a huge old church—but it was too late. We rattled across a plateau ringed with mountains, passing, first, a solitary, most ornate and many-finialed Spanish abbey which was falling to bits in the fields, followed soon by a lake, from which our passing sent up a cloud of wildfowl; then all was emptiness. This high windy place made us think of the Central Asian plateau, with the Pamirs looming, though none of us have been there; a stage on the Silk Road, perhaps ... As we ascended, Salkantay appeared beyond the nearest ranges in a gleaming cluster of peaks; then the three heights of Huanay, now conquered and familiar; and, at last, the unnamed and all-but defeated summit above Two Rivers. Like telescopes opening in collusion with our increasing height, they became taller and more impressive at every loop in the road until we toyed with the fancy that they hated letting us out of sight and were stretching higher and higher to say goodbye ... We bumped through village after village. In one of them a stream was spanned by a beautiful Spanish bridge adorned with four rough-hewn obelisks with stone balls on the top, one of them smashed off. Then we were in a high pass looking down into the basin of mountains whose bottom is filled by the city of Cuzco. It looked magnificent. Domes, cupolas and bell-towers clustered round plazas. The sea of tiles was pierced by patios and the double- and triple-tiered cavities of cloisters piled up round their stone fountains and their wells.

We passed our parish church of Nuestra Señora de Belén—we are fiercely imbued with *esprit du quartier*, now that Cuzco has become so familiar—then on down the steep and Indian-crowded Calle de Belén to the door of the dear old Conquistador. The manager and all the waiters rushed out and all but embraced us. While our stuff was being humped up to our rooms, they filled us up with *pisco* sours on the house.

The bliss of finding clean shirts! Only Robin and Renée's room has an actual *bath*; all the rest are showers; so we wallow there in turn. There was a lot of cheerful bedroom-drinking. The day ended with a mad polyglot dinner in a Chinese restaurant lined with snug curtained alcoves, to entertain our various benefactors, including the Mehders and Don J who was pleased to learn that both the secret police and the bandits had been discreet to the point of invisibility. The feast became comical, boisterous, and totally out of hand.

CUZCO   August 19

The last bit of this letter was written on the patio of an old house, now a museum, which was once the home of Inca Garcilaso de la Vega. He was a strange, rather marvellous figure. His father was a Conquistador from Estremadura, and his mother was an Inca princess and a niece of the penultimate Emperor. When she was a little girl she had escaped being massacred by the last usurping Inca, Atahualpa, who was himself cruelly and perfidiously executed by Pizarro. He wrote a fascinating history of Inca Peru and died in Spain. He is buried somewhere among that forest of columns in Cordoba Cathedral.

Then I moved to the cloister of the Monastery of the Mercéd but didn't get much writing done, owing to the eerie counter-attraction exerted by the murals with which the inner wall of the cloister is frescoed. These are the life-cycle of San Pedro Nolasco, who I'd like to know much more about. (I'll write to Gerald Brenan.) He was a warlike thirteenth-century Catalan noble. In one of the early frescoes he is piously persecuting the Albigensians in Provence. Soon he is founding the Mercederian Order, some of whom later accompanied Columbus and took root in the New World. (They wear white habits, in which half-Indian monks still flit about the cloisters.) Then he visits the Pope, and ransoms Spanish prisoners from the Moors in Cordoba. Later, captured by the Moors and trussed with barbed wire, he is tied on a donkey's back and scourged by wicked turbaned figures through the streets of Moorish Granada. Many adventures ensue, only to be fragmentarily construed in the flaking frescoes and the half-effaced texts in a cartouche at the bottom of each panel.

In spite of S. Pedro's date, all the figures wear Jacobean costume, contemporary with the painter. In one of the last squares, preceding his death and apotheosis, the haloed grey-beard kneels at the BVM's feet, while she, a starry Infanta, offers one breast to the Infant Jesus while the Saint's lips close on the other, his eyelids reverently lowered.

There is a puzzling and perhaps unique feature in all paint-ings of the Trinity by artists of the Cuzco school. The figures of the Trinity are three handsome and identical young men with corn-coloured beards. (The only time I've seen anything similar was in that cave on the top of Mount Autore, on the way to the Abruzzi, where all the peasants and all the beggars for a hundred miles assemble on the vigil of the feast of the Trinity. There, the three figures frescoed in a cave are mild old men with white beards, comfortably seated on a cloud like a sofa.) Some of these Cuzco school paintings are fasci-nating. One series, recently moved from a church and now in the Bishopric (a former nobleman's palace on Inca foun-dations), depicts a ceremonial procession for the feast of Corpus Christi in the seventeenth century; parrots flutter and perch, hidalgos in Carolean costumes mingle with Inca princes adorned with gold discs, plumes, fringes and embroidered suns. There are other historically arresting pictures in the Jesuit Church of the Compañia, painted, as they say, by mestizo hands. In one of them, Don Beltran Garcia de Loyola is being married to a local lady; another shows the marriage of Don Martin de Loyola to an Inca princess descended from the emperors, but now a Christian: Doña Beatriz Ñusta. He is in splendid Spanish attire, she in full Inca regalia. The inscription says that the groom is not only a nephew of S. Ignatius Loyola, but also a member of the Borgia family—Borja, in

Spanish—thus, a sort of great nephew of Cesare and great-great nephew of Alexander VI. I long to know how these strange genes combined. Where are their chief modern descendants? I see, with my mind's eye, a swarthy dinner-jacketed figure murmuring 'No trumps, partner' in the country club in Lima . . .

I haven't said nearly enough about this wonderful town. We leave tomorrow and, I suppose, one will never see it again. I'll get as many guide- and picture-books as I can and take you on a conducted tour *in absentia*. We've only a few hours left, so I'll chuck this for the moment and dash round the town for a last, valedictory look. Tomorrow we go ten hours by train to Lake Titicaca, where we plan to wander along the banks, perhaps camping, and perhaps fishing for those yard-long trout that swim in it. (*Can* this be true?)

P.S. Also love from all your pals here.

P.P.S. We arc just off to see some Quechua dancing and music, which I bet will be a touristic farce. But, as the Chorus in *Henry V* says, judge true things by what their mockeries be.

Now that the climbing is over we are all absolutely acclimatized. I feel as if I'd been breathing the air of Cuzco—that oxygen tent the Quechuas call the sky—all my life. We are all lithe, hatchet-faced, eagle-eyed, masterful, treading like panthers and ready to shin up Kanchenjunga before breakfast.

Third Letter

Third Letter

A STRUGGLE to catch up! I got a wad of stuff posted off in Cuzco, on the afternoon of the 19th, describing our adventures there and in the high Andes—not that we're out of them now. So I'll charge on regardless from where I left off.

*   *   *

When we left the Conquistador that evening, the streets were seething. A giant student demonstration-procession-rag was afoot, connected with the opening of a new school. There had been some riots and arrests and overturned cars earlier on, unloosed by the Government's replacement of the Rector of the University. But this one seemed all in fun, a half-orderly, half-rowdy pageant with innumerable brass and jazz bands: mummers, pantomime horses with two people under a cloth, mock funerals, students in rather sinister skull masks, troops of skeletons, a grotesque honeymoon-couple in a ges-tatorial double bed, boys with donkey's ears, fat people padded out to enormous girth, bottle-wielding drunkards, dragoons waving sabres, turnip-lanterns on poles, dandies in battered opera hats, plumed Incas, life-size chessmen and

63

cowled familiars of the Holy Office. The not very bright street lamps turned it into a Goya scene, and when we had fought our way through it and run down empty backstreets, we found the colonnaded Plaza de Armas a mass of banked humanity. Indian boys had scaled the façades of all the churches in the plaza including the Cathedral. They huddled in the scallop-topped niches, twined themselves among the ecstatic cross-bearing saints and clung like swarming bees among the alternating obelisks and bell-shaped finials of the entablature. You've never seen so many Quechua Indians assembled since the fall of the Incas: a forest of ponchos and panama-tophats and different coloured bowlers and those wonderful red, green, yellow and blue embroidered hats like upside-down mushrooms or macaroons. It was all very mild and friendly. Later on, there was a vague fizzle and pop of fireworks, gentle as a rushlight compared to those glorious debauches in Italy. Indians are anticlimactic, patient and utterly unjadeable. They were still quietly swarming, two hours later, when, full of wine and chicken *à la Creole*, we struggled back to the Conquistador. The siren and the prairie-sounding bell of the night train rang through our bedrooms for the last time.

PUNO, ON LAKE TITICACA (11,400 feet above sea-level)
August 20

Kind to the last, our Swiss benefactors, Herr Mehder and his wife from the Cervezeria Cuzqueña, drove us to the station at 7 a.m. They were urgent with warnings about dishonest pseudo-porters. Parties of young Indians, they say, pretend to fight over the passengers' luggage, and then make off with it in the confusion.

The train was almost as charming as the one from Delhi to Agra. There was a delicious breakfast of bacon and eggs, and later a huge luncheon ushered in by vodka and washed down with Chianti. The railway followed valleys and gorges between steep sierras, continuously climbing from the already exalted height of Cuzco, to emerge at last on a sparsely vegetated tableland that lifted us, with a straining groan at every turn of the wheel, to an invisible watershed at 13,330 feet. Down the otherwise imperceptible slope the other side, the wheels suddenly began to turn more briskly. The region is interchangeably known as the Altiplano, the Puna, and the Sierra. It is a wide, high prairie of lonely haciendas speckled with cattle and flocks. Herds of llamas and alpacas loiter across the landscape, all twisting their long necks to peer at us as we clattered past. The scene took on a rather dismal aspect in the early sunset. We thought romantically that it was just the place, if we were a thousand miles further north, for a sudden howling troop of Chipaways in full warpaint to stampede alongside and fill us with arrows . . . The last streaks of daylight vanished while we halted in a stricken town called Juliaca. What a place to be consul in.

An hour later, we shunted into the desolation of Puno on the now invisible shores of Lake Titicaca. Here, as we had been warned, a swarm of Aymara Indian boys ran wild, seizing our luggage and bickering and punching each other all the way across the tracks to the repellent Ferrocarril Hotel, where chaos and congestion reigned. Robin had reserved rooms a day before by telephone; but they had never heard of us, and there were no rooms. A small boy, left on duty, must have taken the message and forgotten to report it; at least so said one of the horrible receptionists, with a triumphant gnash of gold teeth. Worse still, Robin's kitbag, stuffed with indispensable gear and cameras and binoculars, was missing. He and I went to search for it at the station. We drew a blank in our empty carriage, now in a siding. There was nothing but a pat on the shoulder and a few '*¡Que barbaridads!*' from the Norfolk-jacketed *Jefe*, which died away in a diminuendo of shrugs. We headed glumly for the Stacion de la Guardia Civil. This led us past the revolting Ferrocarril, where André dashed out: the missing kitbag had been found!—in the chaos, it had been taken to another hotel, and he had tracked it down ... I mustn't spin out the horrors of Puno. Our wails and threats finally extorted two rooms like Black Holes of Calcutta. We dossed down three in each. They had immovable frosted interior windows, with not only no hot water (in pretentious hotels, this had become a bit of a fetish with us after the joyfully accepted rigours of the mountains) but no water at all, for faces, teeth, chins or anything, in spite of the mocking taps and chains. By cockcrow the vile place was fetid with fifty impacted privies. We washed our teeth from a half-empty soda-water bottle found in an empty bar and burst into the fresh air like djinns out of a bottle.

There was little for the eye to feast on outside. Puno is an assembly of corrugated iron roofs, sidings and goods yards sprawling round a church like a Gothic mud pie. We picked a way through the debris and the squatting Aymara Indians— treading softly lest we trod on their dreams— to a ramshackle lacustrine port where an old steamer lay at anchor, brought piecemeal overland long before the railway, so that each plate was cut down to the weight a mule can carry, and sometimes a llama, then welded and riveted together again on the lake shore. At last, we were standing on the edge of Lake Titicaca, glittering and enormous under a pale sky. It's the highest navigable water in the world and seventy-one times the size of Lake Lucerne. Soon we were chugging across it in a small motor boat.

This part of the lake was semi-enclosed by two peninsulas; in the middle distance beyond them, it spread almost like the open sea. A wide channel led us between reedy sandbanks. Hundreds of ducks and some birds like moorhens, others like pintails, and yet other smaller russet creatures with black heads and sky-blue beaks, were wandering about or on the wing. More sky-blue beaks were attached to much larger grey birds, and on the rushes perched blackbirds wearing yellow epaulettes.

We were heading for an archipelago of floating islands where the descendants of the Uru Indians live. 'These', so a guide book says, 'claim to be sub-human.' This unique boast gains in substance when one meets them. We were soon surrounded by their *balsas*—unsinkable gondola-like canoes of solid and densely plaited straw—then we landed on one of their islands. These thick artificial rafts are an acre or more wide, and constructed like the *balsas*. The huts are lopsided straw-matting bivouacs. It is very shallow here, and though they are linked now by vegetation to the lake's bottom, storms sometimes carry the islands far from their fragile moorings. Here the happy analphabetics live hugger-mugger among the waving reeds on an acrid and waterlogged humus of trodden straw and mud and fish-scales and droppings, rather like colonies of gannets. In exchange for boxes of matches and bread-rolls they offered us artless and unpretentious embroideries: rags of canvas on which pink, crimson and green golliwogs with their arms projecting like twigs had been unambitiously stitched in thick wool, as though by three-year-old Mirós. I wish I'd bought one. I've never seen artefacts less corrupted. The last pure Urus, it seems, died out about fifteen years ago, and these are their hybrid descendants. They are Seventh Day Adventists, and the whole community was converted from paganism *en masse* ten years ago in a brilliant apostolate lasting half a morning.

Wings whirl everywhere in the rustling reeds. Mirages turn the other, solid, islands of the lake, by seeming to undercut them, into Laputas that hover over the flashing waste; and all round the horizon, reminding us of the enormous altitude, the tops of cumulus clouds come cauliflowering up from below. There is a mad feeling of dimensionless vacancy in the air. Sunstroke hovers. Our engine gave out on the way back to Puno and we were only saved from helplessly drifting and going insane with the glare by the arrival of a large and roughly built *caique*, in whose path we happened to be. It was manned by fifty Aymara Indians from the solid island of Taquile: cheerful, friendly, shy, bronze-faced and horsehair-tressed people, all of them nursing bundles of humble produce and nets full of salt fish for the Puno market. Some of the women were hatted in the familiar bottle-green bowler. Others wore flexible mortar-boards of brown felt embroidered with silk in patterns of delicate Aubusson-like flowers of the greatest subtlety. These hats were perched on the top of black shawls which covered their heads and shoulders and gave them an air of Venetian ladies painted by Longhi and only those bird-beaked masks were missing. The skirts were psychedelic in colour, russet, shocking pink, electric green and scarlet, and each was adorned halfway down with a thick flounce and worn over many petticoats. There were bodices— or rather, cloth breast-plates lacing down the sides—as intricately worked as the Aubusson mortar-boards. They were very different from the tattered Uru amphibians we had just left. The men passed round bottles of *pisco* and *chicha*, while the women span with distaffs and spindles. Sitting on the decked-in prow we lolled and gazed in a tangled and luxurious coma between sleeping and waking until the keel grounded among the reeds of Puno.

Finding a truck we fled the terrible town. Heading south along the lake, we crossed miles of rolling country scattered with purple upheavals of rock in the shapes of leaning blades and brontosaurs and pan-pipes. The lake might have been the sea; a few peninsulas dimly projected, and far away, beyond the invisible eastern shore, and already in Bolivia, the glaciers of the Cordillera Real flashed in mid-air. We bumped through half a dozen dusty little towns and drew up on the banks of the Rio Llave. It is very wide. One of the spans of the bridge had fallen in and the current rushed along like a North African *oued* in spate. We crept across it up to our axles in the flood, while a team of llamas gazed down from the bank with disapproval. We reached our destination, the town of Juli, about dusk. Below the little town stood some impressive baroque ruins, dimly perceived in the twilight. The Plaza Hotel was isolated in a dip between the lakeside hills about two furlongs from the shore. It looked rather nice, in an ultra-modern way; our spirits rose at the thought of a luxurious sojourn that would erase the memory of the Ferrocarril.

In vain! There by the door an enormous charabanc was disgorging a staunchless flow of middle-aged Australian and

New Zealand tourists, bear-led by a dapper young Englishman in an RAF blazer; all with rooms booked months before. Thank God, Robin had fixed up ours, we thought. But the manager, whom we had met and made the arrangements with in Puno, hadn't turned up. Chaos reigned; the electric current was off; the two Indian waiters were in a state of demoralization; everyone sat in desolate groups in the shadows. The lights came on finally and we cheered up a bit, after making them start an enormous log-fire; anywhere beyond its radius was like a frigidaire. To keep cold and gloom at bay, sweaters and duvets were hauled out and whisky poured. Of course, the hotel people had never heard of us and every bed was taken. After an unimaginative meal, we went to bed on the floor in sleeping-bags on top of sofa-cushions, reading for a bit by candlelight, for it was dark again. An unkinder cut was in store: the highest navigable waterway in the world lay just under the windows and there was not a drop of water in the pipes, either hot or cold.

Flashback

After sunset on the bleakest evening at Goose Tarn, I remembered one of Goya's *Caprichos*, depicting half a dozen misshapen creatures huddling on a dark and desolate plain with a few sinister streaks of daylight in the east. Goya had written underneath: '*¡Si amanece, nos vamos!*'—'If dawn breaks, we go!' It might have been us. Robin recalled another from the *Horrors of War* at the Goya exhibition at Burlington House, showing four soldiers brawling. The legend underneath was translated as 'Three against one? Stuff his arse with hay!' It was the boldness of the translation that had struck Robin; us too. It's become a catch-phrase, suiting all situations, regardless of relevance. We repeated it now as we blew our candles out and it cheered us up.

JULI, LAKE TITICACA   *August 21*

The Australians and New Zealanders piled into their bus in the small hours and crashed off to the Bolivian border and La Paz. They were very nice, but they hadn't the remotest idea where they were, where they had come from, or where they were going; or even why they were on the move at all. Their English dragoman told us the party had started off at Buenos Aires and would end up at Panama, all at breakneck speed, and scarcely alighting except for food and sleep.

So the hotel is ours. Dozens of rabbits flop about under the French windows and there will clearly be hundreds in a few months' time. I rather like them. Andrew says they give him the creeps. There is a back yard with a few ducks and a number of chickens. Aha! we thought, delicious new-laid eggs for breakfast. We had lent a watch to the Aymara cook with minute instructions about egg-boiling times. But when they turned up an hour later, six groans escaped us: they were either hard as plaster of Paris or soft as slime. Admittedly, the altitude does make a difference to the time needed for boiling; but surely, we moaned to each other, the Aymaras must have discovered *how* long, after their millions of years' incumbency. They're not Urus ... (They are rather nice, especially one called Juan.) In fact, the Aymara are said to be more energetic and quick-witted than the Quechua. Their languages are unconnected, although the Incas, who spoke Quechua, are legendarily supposed to have originated on Lake Titicaca.

The Aymara nation, which stretches far into Bolivia, was only incorporated in the Inca empire about eighty years before the Spanish conquerors arrived. These two races—Sierra or Altiplano Indians—are known as *cholos*. The other Indian groups that inhabit the Montaña—which means the tropic forest region east of the Andes in the Amazon basin—are called *chunchos* or *bárbaros*. They are countless scattered tribes of fishermen and hunters, all of them wild and untouched, who riddle strangers with arrows on sight.

A tall, sinister silhouette came slinking in. *The manager!* Robin and I leaped up to expostulate about the rooms last night and the water today, but our halting Spanish took all the sting out of our curses. He is a lanky, impassive, narrow-moustached ladino with an ironic eye; he merely went on chewing a toothpick, his thumbs stuck in his belt with hands hanging: his irremovable sombrero redundantly shades features already by no means open. He might be a train-robber or a pimp, with a dash of croupier and gaucho thrown in; rather an intriguing figure in an awful way. What graft or nepotism can have landed him in charge of the hotel? The water supply, we learn, comes all the way from Puno; it has broken down all through the province. *Perhaps the manager is king of the Puno underworld ...*

*   *   *

In and near Juli are scattered half a dozen baroque churches in different stages of decay. The pediments on the splendid doorways are doubly broken, and tiers of twin pillars mount the façades. Parasites tuft every ledge and roots break through and tilt the heavy tufa ashlars askew. Only one of all these churches is still in action. It dominates the main plaza and flies the Pope's white and yellow gonfalon with the keys and the tiara. Bowler in hand, a multi-skirted squaw or two mooned about the restored interior. It was Sunday morning, and the place was still redolent with the aftermath of incense. The loins of a crucifix with blood-clotted kneecaps and a dusty wig of red hair were clothed in a pleated kilt of open-work lace. The carnage and convoluted gilding with which the Counter-Reformation filled the new churches of Latin America must have provided some compensation for the takeover in Mexico and Guatemala; and more especially in Peru, where the sun-temples had been lined with sheet-gold, all promptly looted by Pizarro. To people used to human sacrifice—which was much rarer in Peru than Mexico—the Inquisition and the well-staged executions must have made the deprivation less visually abrupt. Conversion was rapid and complete. I wonder if semi-pagan rites are still observed in remote places, as they are in Mexico and Guatemala?

Juli was a Jesuit stronghold, a sort of training ground and springboard for the religious, political and economic takeover of Paraguay. It lasted for the best part of a century and Robin and I wondered if any battered remains of their libraries still survived among the inhabitants; half an hour's wandering in the meagre desolation of the modern town blasted any such hope. An old stone and adobe house in the plaza must have had some secular importance; over the door is a carved, half-effaced shield quartering the arms of Castile and Aragon on the breast of a double-headed Imperial Eagle, which means that it must have been built between Pizarro's entry into Cuzco in 1533 and Charles V's abdication in 1558.

The most beautiful of the ruins lay on the side of a gentle

hill between the town and the lake. A charming ceremonial archway leads into a walled courtyard full of shady trees and we dawdled here for ages, quoting du Bellay and sitting about the broken steps that ascend to a great carved door which looked as though it hadn't opened for years. A rough and engaging decoration of tropical fruit and flowers and vines and, I think, of mermaids and monkeys, jutted in high relief. We stood on tiptoe to peer in through lunettes and chinks at a topsy-turvy upheaval of intruding vegetation slanted with sunbeams from inaccessible windows. Wild flowers and grasses grew in every fissure, and lake-birds perched on the unsteady belfry.

The liveliest bit of modern Juli is a market full of brilliant costumes and stalls packed with fruit and vegetables. Under Renée's direction, we stocked up as though for a siege, returning to the hotel with magnificent spherical cabbages under our arms, and a bagful of lesser trophies. She handed them over to the cook with strict instructions. What about those yard-long trout, we asked the manager. It's no good; fishing has been forbidden for a year; the stock, artificially introduced ten years ago, has been ruthlessly depleted. Andrew was downcast at the news, as he might have caught one and put it among the other eccentric fauna that cover the walls of Pratts. (I forgot to mention that some local mountaineers we met in Cuzco made us a present of two rare stuffed waterfowl from Titicaca that ought to end up in the same pantheon.)[1]

---

[1] They have.

A revolution has broken out in Bolivia. We were told this by a newly-arrived French party in the hotel: a right-wing military coup, it seems, was aimed at the present regime, which is similar, on general lines, to the one in Peru. There has been a lot of shooting and a number of deaths. We had been toying, slightly half-heartedly, with the idea of crossing the border to see the pre-Inca ruins of Tiahuanaco, and perhaps pushing on to La Paz; but it seems unwise, as the border might be closed, holding us up the other side of it for ages; or so they say. The French party consists of two very pretty girls and two men, one of them a tall ambrosially bearded young Burgundian wrapped in a red poncho as ample as a toga. He has just taken a degree in oenology—wine-growing, that is—at Dijon. We sat by the fire and he instructed us about local wines: none of the Peruvian ones are any good; only the contraband Chilean, smuggled into the country over remote passes. We must try and get some. André is sure he must be the owner, or the heir, of a small vineyard in Burgundy.

I forgot to mention that Don J had turned up trumps on that last social evening in Cuzco. During dinner, we said we wanted to try chewing the coca-leaf. Next morning, he arrived from the market with a bundle of the very best, he said, and a ball of the grey potash that has to be chewed simultaneously. The leaves are circular and quite small. I tried one, chewed away for a bit, then spat it out. Renée and Robin have made a more dutiful and persevering attempt; they munched for a few minutes and then, sadly, tailed off too. Perhaps it's only after the second day's steady grinding that the real beauty begins to dawn.

JULI August 22

Water has started arriving at the hotel! Now comes the uphill struggle for heating it. It's a challenge.

There was no progress with the eggs at breakfast. Sighs and groans burst out all round. They might have been those china eggs used for darning or slipped into coops to make poultry lay.

Except for Andrew, who's got some tummy trouble, we set off south along the lake's shore, and trudged for miles over the sand and the pebbles. It was very calm and beautiful: cliffs and grassy hills, and, every hundred paces or so, swarms of waterfowl which flew out over the lake at our approach and then settled in busy throngs a hundred paces further, until we put them on the wing again. We ate our picnic under cliffs riddled with bird-sheltering holes, and watched the hovering and circling of a beautiful grey hawk. The lake is a sparkling expanse surrounded by low white clouds under a very pale sky. Again, that Andean phenomenon: not a drop of sweat, in spite of the heat and the glare: it is all scorched away by the dryness.

When we neared home shadows were falling and an icy breath followed their advance across the low hills; then the cold bit to the bone. Robin and Renée, who had lagged behind peering at the birds through glasses, caught us up with a report of three almost legless, ferret-like animals, twice as long as foxes, scuttling through the grass.

★   ★   ★

Juan announced hot water! There was an immediate dash to

our rooms; after running cold for five minutes, it became tepid for two, then returned to cold for ever.

We found Andrew hobnobbing with a very good-looking (and very nice) Austrian woman, dashingly clad in trousers and a belted jersey, with a tall shaggy, rather nice son, on holiday from Munich with a girlfriend. She has lived in Peru—in Arequipa, our next destination—for twenty years and loves it. We all huddled, rugged up to the neck, round the blazing logs, whisky in hand. I think Mrs Lang (who is actually a Croatian from Zagreb—her *husband* is Austrian) finds us a bit childish and spoilt to go on so about the hot water and the unimaginative food (the vegetables at dinner had all been boiled down to a nearly invisible uniform pulp). *Ah yes*! we come back like a flash, but this is a new, ultra-modern, fairly expensive hotel, and if *everyone* grins and bears it in silence, the place will welter in error and sloth for ever. We've got her there. While we talked, the sombreroed manager came and leant against the door with legs and arms akimbo and thumbs belt-slung in that *pistolero*'s stance of his. He eyed us for a few minutes, then lounged away, as though late for an ambush or an assassination. 'What an extraordinary man!' Mrs Lang said.

They say the fighting is getting worse in Bolivia; but it's all rumour, as no papers seem to get here. (We have become ardent readers of *El Comercio* and *La Prensa*.)

JULI August 23

When we first arrived, we tried to arrange for a team of horses to take our camping stuff, or just ourselves, down the lake shore for a day or two. But nothing happened in spite of our repeated pleas. This morning two moderate animals turned up, howdah-ed in conquistadorish saddles with high pommels and wooden bucket-stirrups. Robin and I tittupped into Juli to find more vegetables, and provisions for a picnic. We passed Mrs Lang driving her small brood off to Arequipa in a Landrover and gave her a hidalgo-ish flourish with our battered headgear.

When shadows fall, the place becomes not only very cold, but also slightly sinister. Wind ruffles the grey surface of the lake, the rabbits scuttle and bound in the gloaming. One of them got indoors this evening; I swear they have multiplied since our arrival. When Juan came in before dinner with a cry of '*¡Agua caliente!*' we headed more warily to our lustral areas, and it really was hot. Blithely, I was under the shower in a flash, but just as I had become a white pillar of soapy lather it went ice cold again ... Perfect timing. Agued and shivering, we crept back defeated to the fireside. There was a gleam of triumph in the manager's eye under his hat-brim, as he sauntered past ... I forgot to mention that the eggs, at breakfast, had swung back to liquid ... He's two up, now.

JULI August 24

We gathered fatalistically round the breakfast table. A couple of taps with our spoons revealed the predictable truth: they were hard as stones again.

Then a wonderful thing happened. Maddened with frustration, Robin let out a scarcely audible gasp of 'O G-god!' Then, rising from his chair with blue eyes ablaze, he picked up the fossilized missile and flung it the length of the dining-room. It bounded from ceiling to wall and scattered in a thousand fragments.

For a moment, all were aghast. Then hilarity broke out. Had the manager seen this bold act through the glass door and realized he was beaten? Andrew is convinced that a spell has been broken and that our luck turned at that moment. A look of wonder and respect, not far removed from love, was kindled in the eyes of Juan and the other Indians. The manager, all officious pliancy now, eagerly rushed up with the news of a fascinating Indian ceremony a few miles away. Yes, but how could we get there? Nothing easier: his brother had a *camionette* and would drive us there. If we wanted six horses tomorrow, he was sure they could be found! Alas, we were leaving the next day; but what about the *camionette*? The manager was off on his motor bike like the wind and the Aymara cook was standing by to consult us about dinner. What about those ducks in the back yard, we said. Ducks? By all means! In a moment he was heading for the back yard, knife in hand ...

The *pistolero*'s brother was a lively, cheerful chap. We piled into his battered shooting-brake. Pictures of St. Christopher, Che Guevara, and the Scourging of Christ were glued to the windscreen. He was a wild driver and he just missed an oncoming bus. Swooping past the wreck of another which lay upside down and buckled like a concertina, he blithely told us that seven people had been killed in it the week before, including a Frenchman and a Belgian girl. There are more deaths per mile on Peruvian roads, he added with sombre pride, than anywhere else in the world.

We drew up at the bottom of a steep hill where Indians were converging in hundreds. The women were clad in their bowlers and psychedelic multiple skirts, but many of the men were in curious fancy dress: tailcoats with silver buttons, high collars, Anthony Eden hats, false noses, goggles, white gloves and identical closed umbrellas stripped of cloth, so that only spokes remained; the wide pink ribbons of an imaginary order ran across their shirt-fronts. *Diplomaticós* or *magistrados*, we were told. They looked extremely creepy. There were others in bell-like copes of gold, silver, pink and sky-blue brocade; facsimiles, they said, possibly rather fancifully, of pre-Spanish religious vestments. (They are unlike any of the costumes in those Cuzco pictures; but then, they are Aymara.) Some of these caparisoned people wore headgear like Tantric devil-masks fitted with fangs, tusks, spiralling horns, lolling tongues and eyes as big as cricket-balls that rolled loose in their sockets. Two silver bands—big drums and flashing bassoons so enormous that, except for their scuttling legs, the players were totally concealed—were climbing beside us. The crowd grew denser as we approached the top.

The steep zigzag through the rocks is a Way of the Cross, and every pilgrim laid a pebble on the plinth of each successive cross as he passed it. The last Station stands outside a little stone chapel on the summit. It is dedicated to Saint Bartholomew, whose feast day it was, and the rough stone pen round the shrine was crammed. When the brief Mass was over, out came a young American priest in a scarlet chasuble, followed by a retinue of demons and mummers. He was very handsome, with corn-coloured hair and beard, and twice the height of any of his flock. After delivering a homily in Spanish, he dipped an aspergill and sprinkled the silent penned throng.

We were beckoned inside a perfect circle of dolmen-like stones, about the size of a threshing-floor, and were soon sitting on the ground out of the wind, all our legs pointing to the centre, and eating coloured biscuits while an Indian came round with glasses of, unexpectedly, Peruvian champagne; then a tot of whisky; then a slug of *pisco*. Were they right to change so often? (Five thousand *cholos* can't be wrong.) The priest, now in blue jeans and sandals, a blue pullover and an open shirt, had broken the ice with us, as he'd forgotten to bring any cigarettes with him. Flinging back his *pisco*, he said they would probably move on to *chicha* next, then to a local spirit, like *aguardiente*, and by nightfall they would all be reeling. He seemed pleased at meeting the only other fellow gringos for a moment in this *cholo* maelstrom. He loves the Aymara and said one mustn't believe all their detractors say (*What's that?* we wondered). He had been here a year and a half, and was beginning to speak Aymara, which made a great difference.

I bet this strange circle—a closer-knit sawn-off Stonehenge—existed long before the chapel. It was filling to bursting point. A neighbouring Indian couple, cumbered with other offspring, put André and me in charge of two minute twins called Rafael and Xavier: they were rather like Japanese dolls, with straight, thick blue-black hair in a fringe. All this time, the two silver bands had been pounding away non-stop at a tune almost identical to *Little Brown Jug don't I love thee*. Outside the sacred circle, we caught sight of Andrew and Carl, whom we had lost, towering high over a sea of bowlers. But no beckoning could lure them inside this Royal Enclosure: perhaps it was shyness, or too much like Social Life. The middle of the circle was cleared, a table with a vase of plastic flowers whisked away, and those blackclad *magistrados* or *diplomaticós* trooped in. They began a grave, shuffling and, as it turned out, interminable dance. Repetition holds no terrors here. It was speeded up every so often by a faster pirouette as each *diplomaticó* pivoted on his disquieting skeleton umbrella, all their Anthony Edens lifting in unison. There was something not only disturbing but reminiscent about those black glasses and long noses and sombre clothes ... Then I remembered! They were like a troop of Guédés, myrmidons of the God of the Cemeteries in Haitian Voodoo and followers of Baron Samedi.[1]

After a long session, we extracted ourselves with a ceremonious circle of handshakes, and joined Carl and Andrew. The half acre of wind-swept hilltop was now packed. Smaller circles of those multiple skirts revolved and bobbed in time to the bands, the slung babies bounced up and down, fast asleep; and jovial lurching showed that drink was not being swallowed in vain. Peering over the edge, we saw the hillside was still dark with clambering *cholos*. Soon there would hardly be standing room; one could imagine festive figures rolling down the slope, all the way to the lake's shore, and in. But all these activities were oddly quiet; anywhere else the noise would have been deafening. Below, Lake Titicaca streamed away like a sheet of mercury. It was wreathed by a garland of cumulus and Bolivian glaciers gleamed across the whole eastern horizon. It was a platform in the sky where the bronze-faced throng would twirl and lurch in impassive ecstasy till the sun set. We slipped away.

When the notes of the bands died down, we found ourselves treading in exhilaration through wide and sweet-smelling dales. The hills soared and subsided towards faraway blue

[1] See *The Traveller's Tree*, chapter 11.

triangles of the lake. We crossed the landscape, each at his own pace, meeting nobody all day except a small and friendly shepherd playing a wooden flute, and an even smaller shepherdess. It was as bare of vegetation as one of the Lesser Cyclades; empty of everything but sunlight, dazzling air, flocks, birds and aromatic shrubs—hard to stop singing as one flew from height to height. We ate our bread and chocolate in an alcove of rock almost inside the lake, where the water-birds stood in the lee of a wooded cliff. After a spell of torpor, we climbed the cliff again, and wandered all the afternoon along winding tracks hemmed in by low walls towards the dip in the mountains where Juli lay. Strips of plough-land sloped to the cliffs' edge and the stubble fields turned to gold. We passed one or two lonely estancias in spinneys of eucalyptus and umbrella pine, and as we approached our own hollow by the shore, the chill shadow of dusk swept across the lake and the hills. Suddenly Carl, his ears sharpened by half a lifetime in the Alps, stopped and said 'Listen!' There was a faint vibration in the air. It resolved itself, as we strained our ears, into the barely audible throbbing of the tune that had scanned the whole morning. *Little Brown Jug*, far, far away. A last sunbeam, slanting nearly horizontal for leagues from a mountain cleft, struck the crest of the chapel-hill and picked out the flash of a silver bassoon, a big drum's disc, the gleam of a trombone. The hilltop heaved with just discernible motion . . .

The windows of the hotel were twinkling just ahead. We went in, to find—

Ah, what? Juan, all smiles. In dead silence he led each of us to our rooms, and turned on the taps: out rushed a steaming jet! Half an hour later we gathered glowing round the huge fireplace and called for drinks in voices hushed with wonder. The manager flitted benignly across the middle distance smiling like a kind bandit in an opera. When we sat down to dinner, in came an enormous duck, piping hot, done to a turn, and embedded in a whole orchestra of delicious vegetables ...

We retire exhausted but happy. It has been a wonderful day. We are leaving tomorrow in the manager's brother's *camionette*. I'm inclined to agree with Andrew. Our luck changed (touch wood!) in that infinitesimal moment of destruction and creation when the shell of Robin's flung egg made contact with the dining-room ceiling.

PUNO   August 25

At breakfast, our six eggs were heart's desire.

As the manager's brother's truck was late in arriving, he set off on his motor bike to see what had happened. A bit later, the rumour of an accident reached the hotel. (How? There's no telephone.) Juan went off, turning up two hours later with another truck and the appalling news that the manager's brother had been overturned in his *camionette* and killed outright. He told us all this with a quiet smile, as though it were a regrettable event, but not unusual. We longed to do something about the manager—our feelings had changed since yesterday, and even if they hadn't ... But what? '*¡Vamos!*' the driver kept urging. So, leaving our condolences, we set off in a very subdued frame of mind. We couldn't help thinking, too, that, if it hadn't been for his fatal accident, we would be whirling back to Puno with the poor chap at the wheel ...

We jolted through the boulders of the Rio Llave again,

still axle-deep in rushing water, and on through that curious landscape with the strange outcrops of stone. We stopped for a quarter of an hour in a little town—Acora? Chicuita?—with a stone fountain and an elaborate sundial and a pillar where the heads of executed felons were once displayed. A baroque church rose from a balustraded terrace where a tall wooden cross was embedded in a stone socket. These outdoor calvaries have no figure on them; instead, all the adjuncts of the Passion are arranged in a V-shaped panoply: the lance, the reed with the vinegar-sponge, the ladder, the nails, the lantern, the cup of Gethsemane, the hammer, the pincers, and some-times the curved sword with the soldier's ear still stuck to the blade: but there is always a length of white cloth—the Shroud, or the cloth used in the Deposition?—looped from the middle of each arm of the cross-bar, with the ends hanging loose and fluttering discoloured by dust and frayed by the wind.

The notes of a brass band came down a side street into the plaza, soon followed by the instruments themselves and a slowly whirling circle of dancers. The many-petticoated skirts, pleated and bell-shaped in repose, flared out like carnations as they revolved. It was a wedding, bottles were passing from hand to hand without breaking the step and all the dancers, including the bride and the groom, were very unsteady, but the slow, lurching nature of the dance came to their rescue. Following their example we passed a bottle round the dusty interior during the remaining kilometres to Puno.

The corrugated-iron roofs shone brighter as we approached the hell-town. But what a change from the Ferrocarril was our new hotel! Charming rooms, carved wooden beds, and baths that worked; stuffed herons and flamingos perched benevolently about the hall and the saloons; a beckoning bar

... Here we learnt, from some people who had just come from La Paz, that the Bolivian revolution was over. Major Hugo Banzer, the head of the military junta, had seized power and the overthrown President Torres had fled to Lima for asylum. Many were killed and wounded in the south—several hundred, it seems—and a girl told how she had crouched in a chemist's shop while random bursts of fire smashed all the bottles on the shelves overhead. The new government is extremely right-wing, the late one fairly left, more or less in line with the Peruvian regime which, in spite of the arbitrary land reforms which the landowners naturally consider outright Communism, is said to be still to the right of the Allende government in Chile. It's not very easy to get the hang of.

A huge taxi drove us north this afternoon into a wide loose-knit landscape of prairie and hills. We passed a few flocks, a derelict Spanish church, a hacienda embowered in a wood and, every now and then, a solitary horseman. Branching from the main road, we followed a series of twists and turns that brought us to Lake Umayo. Above the salt-crusted shore rose the steep peninsular bluff of Sillustani. Its back bristled with a scattering of the strange buildings we had come to see. They are called *chullpas*: beautifully built cylinders of large, carefully squared and cambered stone, standing among the rocks and the squat vegetation. At their base they are several yards—four? five?—in diameter, but the girth of the cylinders expands as they ascend, until, about six or seven yards up, a band of masonry projects six inches in a taenia half a yard wide; two more feet end in the cylinder's flat top; from here, when we had clambered up by gaps between the slabs, we could look down into cylindrical interiors choked with masonry and boulders. They were burial places of caciques of the Aymara in pre-Inca times. Originally, they were full of bones and skeletons and mummies, probably the remains of widows and concubines. The place was an isolated congeries of small granite gasometers. Below the bluff on which they stood were two well-cut disc-like platforms of stone several yards across—rather like the stylobate of the tholos of Athene Pronoia at Delphi—drained by runnels that reminded me of those Maya sacrificial stones at Copan: *what for?* ... We climbed up again to the enigmatic cylinders. On the other side of this bluff lay a much larger expanse of this volcanic lake hemmed in by an upheaval of bare hills with a flat-topped island in the centre. A fierce wind blew up suddenly, thrashing the lake into angry waves and whistling through the scrub and the *chullpas*; it was so strong that we could hardly stand. The place was desolate and sinister in the extreme. Renée, the most balanced of people, confessed later that she had felt overcome by the atmosphere; almost, she said, as if she were going to faint. Baleful influences were about. On the way back loops of shadow were advancing across the pampas. Solitary herons stood about in the stubble-fields.

Andrew and I took turns in the luxuriously hot bath next to our room; then went down to the little bar with its stuffed flamingos for *pisco* sours and whiskies and soda. The streets and pavements were fringed with Indian market-people crouched in a coma, or asleep. Groups huddled round braziers which glowed in the dark like nomads' fires on a steppe. The nondescript figures of all nationalities that filled the Lago restaurant turned it into an eating-hell in the Klondyke during the gold rush: the meal was rather good, except for the deafening piped music. On our last visit, two ponchoed and picturesque mestizo tarts hung about the bar with carefree blandishments; but, to our disappointment, they failed to show up tonight. The wine was terrible; but we managed to get hold of some smuggled Chilean.

AREQUIPA *August 26*

This morning the train climbed from the lake up the same track which had brought us in the dark from Cuzco. At the dismal junction-town of Juliaca, we branched south and a wonderful ascent began: through rolling pampas of organ-cactus and savannah at first, where large herds of llamas and alpacas roamed; up; up; until all was bare, and the railway was coiling among bald peaks striped with patches of snow. Deep and tortuous lakes evolved alongside us; the air grew thinner and sharper every minute. (It was the highest railway in the world, someone said; but I believe it is only the second highest, ceding first place to the line to Quito.) Friendly Indian stewards brought us a splendid lunch and we munched and sipped in the sky. Once again, Robin, André and Carl had their altimeters on the table, and at last, at the height of over 13,000 feet, the slow grind of the wheels changed to the brisker downhill note; another watershed had been crossed ... The track unwound through a desert of interlocking hills and lakes riven by deep gullies that widened into canyons and zigzagged away into the distance. Lower down, the landscape turned to dust and ashes and the conical volcano of Misti soared into the sky. Finally, we were racing across a plateau. A warning straggle of suburbs sprang up, an aerodrome with a windsock, then a factory; finally a bridge carried us over a rushing and boulder-strewn river into Arequipa.

This lovely town is entirely built of white tufa blocks cut from the volcano which dominates the city. Earthquakes have destroyed the place again and again; each time they build it up with the same material. The worst visitation was in the eighteenth century, and it has more of the feeling of a Spanish town of that date than any we've seen so far; thick arches and vaults and columns and porticoes and balconies surround us. The centre of the town is an immense tiered and arcaded plaza with a fountain in the centre and a cathedral filling one side of it; all in this snowy stone. Like many in Peru, the churches here are fronted with spiralling pillars hoisting a complex variety of pediments, and the façades are recklessly vermiculated with carved detail until they seem to crawl with petrified maggots. They remind one a bit of those buildings in Lecce, all riotously thicketed with detail, built by architects whose names all begin with a Z. The overall impact of the town is magnificent.

There is a sort of Grand Canyon not far away which we thought of trying to fly over in a small aeroplane. It sounds wonderful; but apparently it can't be done, for some reason. Our hotel is a brand new Hispano-Mauresque palace in a leafy suburb. We were very intrigued by a long red wall, over-topped by branches and pierced by a single door with a fanlight: could it be an elaborate, semi-rustic brothel? Gnawed by curiosity, I opened this mysterious threshold and stepped into an overgrown garden with houses dispersed among the trees; a man came out with two enormous and deafening dogs, so I shut it again and vanished. Apparently it is nothing very wicked. It used to belong to a *Tia* something and the houses scattered inside were let to writers—

Noël Coward, among others—for months on end.

In the bar before dinner, we made friends with some American sailors who form a jazz band in a US warship that has dropped anchor in Callao, the port of Lima. One of them was an amusing spectacled Negro from Texas. They were on a sort of goodwill tour of the country.

We dined in a half-Bohemian, half-tourist grotto, festooned with bits, stirrups, saddles, whips, guns and a positive jungle of obsolete equestrian accoutrements. A half-Indian singer howled Neapolitan songs in Spanish down a mike till his veins stood out and the snaffles and curb-chains rattled overhead. The food was marvellous: stuffed maize-pods and peppers and amazing pork roasted on rough grills and accompanied by incendiary red sauce that turned all our mouths into the craters of volcanoes. We swallowed bottle on bottle of wine and great high spirits and much noise ensued: euphoria which lasted all the way back to the hotel, where Robin, Andrew and I, pricking our ears, made a dash for the bar. It was empty except for our musical pals, who were putting on a dazzling performance, purely for their own pleasure: old Dixieland jazz, blues, ragtime. Their skill induced solitary dervishlike dances in their audience of three.

AREQUIPA *August 27*

All this afternoon we wandered round the Convent of Santa Catalina. It's nothing to do with Catiline the conspirator, as one might or mightn't think; it's the Spanish name of St. Catherine of Siena. Enclosed by miles of high, forbidding, snow-white wall, it is a city within a city. Begun in early colonial times, like everything else it must have been shaken down and built up again. Formidable grilled gates lead into a descending series of flagged and cobbled courtyards with fountains and fruit trees. Jutting from the solid baroque core, the painted adobe accretions made it vividly different from the rest of the town; an interplay of blinding white with coarse and marvellous colours. It reminds one of monasteries in Mount Athos or the Greek islands. Some of the cloisters are frescoed with primitive designs of flowers and fruit and animals. It must be the rambling, haphazard, improvised feeling—the open-air laundry, for instance: the enormous tilted amphorae bisected lengthwise, and fed with water through earthenware and tile conduits—which reminds one so compellingly of Vatopedi, the Great Lavra or Patmos. Lanes, alleys and sequestered quarters proliferate like the subdivisions of a town. Parts are boarded off, and 'clausura' is written across the planks; invisible black-and-white Dominican nuns still dwell there in seclusion. Dignified sets of chambers were set aside for abbesses, prioresses and senior nuns—more austere quarters accommodated the younger ones—well supplied with kitchens, private wells and large beds in alcoves. The names of the last incumbents were calligraphically inscribed across the lintels, viz.: La Reverendissima Señora Madre Maria del Pilar Soledad Rosa de las Rosas de Mendoza y Alvarado. Portraits of stern mothers superior, painted by a primitive hand, hang here and there, some with garlands of roses anomalously decking their black-and-white coifs. Vaulted kitchens branch off into brewhouses, store-rooms, still-rooms and pharmacies. Sculleries were filled with arrays of ladles, metal mugs, pannikins, skillets, colanders, dishes, balances, chopping-blocks and cauldrons. Parlours opened into drawing-rooms and minor refectories. I wondered if some bookish young nun, incarcerated there against her will, ever quoted Cicero: '*Quosque tandem abutere, Catilina, patientia nostra?*' Renée said she wouldn't mind being abbess there, clearing out all the tourists and filling it with delightful girls, as of old. I see her point. The place has a curious hushed, insidious charm.

The framed martyrdoms in the main refectory and the mangled crucifix over the Abbess's high table must sometimes have been disturbing at meal times. A long gallery is filled with canvases of the Cuzco and Arequipa schools, which are similar, but not identical. Both of them mingle a Castilian splendour of lace and brocade with a primitive Indian stiffness and everything is spangled with gold stars. There is a terrible life-size mock-up of the Last Supper, the wax and the hair and the velvet deep in dust.

When this monastic city was full, I bet its hierarchy was as follows: a hard nucleus—abbess, prioress, sub-prioress, guest-mistresses, novice-mistresses, librarians and choir-nuns—of austere high-born she-Conquistadors from Castile and Estremadura and perhaps an Inca princess or two, slightly at sea, and all battling for power with the Archbishops of Lima and the Inquisition; gossiping about Madrid and the Viceregal Court, arguing about quarterings and clashing over favourites; or, in their rigorous but splendid retreats, immersed in St. Catherine, St. Teresa or St. John of the Cross and dreaming of mystic marriages and the Stigmata. Then there must have been an army of mestizo lay-sisters, and, finally, swarms of little Quechua and Aymara orphans with their plaits flying as they scuttled everywhere with brooms, laden trays, cordials, covered dishes, medicines and piles of books up to their chins.

*   *   *

All the rest of the day, Mrs Lang, our kind and beautiful Austro-Croatian friend from Juli, drove us from church to church. These were not tormented with elaboration, like the ones I admired and complained of yesterday. Their clear façades, sparse decoration and classical doorways endowed them with a dignified serenity. One in particular, approached from a quiet square, up wide and shallow steps between two obelisks, was entrancing. A low wall enclosed a long, wide, tree-shaded platform of large squares, placed lozenge-wise, of black and white pebbles, and on the far side, up went the church's unencumbered front. (This white volcanic stone often fades to a pale apricot hue, glittering here and there with fragments of quartz, and though it is soft-edged tufa, these fragments make it hard for stonemasons to cut. These symmetrical masses have an airy weightlessness.)

Leaving a shadowy interior, we climbed a hewn staircase to a roof which swelled like a whale's back above the vault of the nave; the cupolas were as shallow as those of a rustic mosque, and the corners were marked by rough-hewn obelisks. We all jumped as a bell, hanging in an open bell-hamper on whose ledge we were sitting, suddenly began to bang out the Angelus ... Biscuit-coloured tiles and towers and tree-tops mingled all round us and beyond them dipped the valley which winds its way south and into Chile. Green patches of cultivated plateau, then waving sierras, joined the tall cone of the volcano, and the pallor of the sky reminded us that we were still very high up. I wonder how we'll all feel at sea-level tomorrow, when we fly back to Lima? We are filled with slight dread and anxiety. Our Peruvian days are numbered.

LIMA   August 28

This morning—our last in Arequipa—we trooped across the town to see the house of Mr Williams, British Consul here for many years, and now, I think, in retirement. When he and his wife bought it, this most beautiful old Spanish house, in a city of beautiful houses, was a total ruin filled with pigs and cattle and choked with muck. The restoration— the flagstones, the patterns of pebbles, the fountains in the courtyards, the crossed vaulting and patios and colonnades, the marvellous white rooms with the carved woodwork and grilles and *azulejos*, and pictures and beautiful Spanish and provincial furniture—is an unalloyed triumph. Ice tinkled in our long drinks in one of the lesser patios as we listened to Mr Williams describing the house's resurrection. He is a delightful man. He's been here fifty years and will never go home now—'Couldn't face that climate—*Brr!*' His ancestors were from Cardiff, but he was born in China—or rather, at sea, off Port Arthur—in the last decade of the nineteenth century. Then we went off to drinks with Mrs Lang and her Austrian husband, who was a very good-looking silver-mining engineer with a delightful manner and white hair that suggested a pianist or perhaps a cardinal. Their garden was full of exotic flowers and trees.

We got into the aeroplane—Colonel Fawcett's dangerously named line again—and headed north-west over endless lesser ranges of the Andes, a tangle of snow-peaks, glaciers and canyons with scattered clouds casting their solitary shadows. The plane swept out over the Pacific and, in a moment, all was cloud. We were inside that all-but permanent pall which hangs over Lima like a cotton-wool tea-cosy for 300 days out of every year. The aerodrome, the slums all the way to Lima, and the streets of the capital itself, were overcast as though a London sky threatened rain. It seems years since we were here.

*   *   *

A body of police were hanging about the entrance to the Alcazar. They carried tommy-guns at the ready and their belts sagged with pistols and sinister black truncheons nearly a yard long. There were more of them indoors, and plain-clothes men lurked in all the passages. Ex-President Torres of Bolivia and several members of the refugee government have moved into all the suites. There has not been a glimpse of them so far.

Our heavy luggage—tents, ice-axes etc.—was waiting for us here, all safely flown from Cuzco, and we soon found Myles Hildyard, back from staying with his brother in Chile and full of tales of Santiago and Valparaiso and the story of the ambassador kidnapped by the Tupamaros in Paraguay. He had been alligator-shooting and we expected the hall of the hotel, and all the rack-space in the homeward-bound aeroplane later on, to be filled with oblong parcels smelling of the swamps; but he had had no luck: they had all been either invisible or out of range. We had a feast of crayfish, lobsters and *loup de mer* at a fashionable restaurant but all of them were rather tasteless, we thought. (Fish and guano are two of the great Peruvian industries. I read in Prescott that the Incas used to plough their terraces with those queer one-man hand-ploughs of hardwood, with a truncated side branch for applying pressure with the foot, which we saw in use on the Altiplano; then they sowed the furrows with sardines to fertilize their maize-fields. Entire mountain ranges must have stunk for leagues. The guano-islands are a snow-white archipelago scattered along the northern coast of Peru, clouded with sea-birds.) Our rooms have turned into a chaos of kitbags, tents, and clothes for the wash.

LIMA   *August 29*

We all feel rather low. It's the anti-climax of being in a large city instead of the space and sky of the last weeks and the physiological reaction of sea-level after the thin mountain air. Acclimatization in reverse, in fact, abetted by the overcast weather. All windscreens are misted with damp from the sea, and the wipers toil non-stop.

Our driver was a half-black; a descendant of the slaves the Spaniards imported to fill up the gaps their policy had made among the Indians. A half-Indian and half-African is called a *zambo*—hence my childhood hero, Little Black Sambo, perhaps. We drove along the Pacific coast through the wilderness of sandhills that surrounds Lima. It is scattered with slums and shanty towns; an ashy waste followed; we might have been driving through half-excavated Cities of the Plain. Rubbish-heaps and the shells of motor cars strewed the landscape. On the edge of this stricken world stands the ruined Inca site of Pachacamac. The pyramids and the half-hewn and half-adobe temples are simultaneously awe-inspiring and dejecting; they were ransacked in vain by Pizarro for fabulous rumoured and still undiscovered hoards. There is none of the splendid decoration of the Maya or the fierce elaboration of the Aztecs. The blank geometrical proliferation is silted up with sand and there is no shade cast by relief or intaglio to rest the eye. Some tame llamas munched miserably in a compound by the little museum. We moved on to a kind of fortified village of ramps and blank walls and courtyards and interior flights of steps and narrow blind passages leading to claustrophobic and windowless chambers. A nightmare. But at least we were back in the sun, outside Lima's dishcover of cloud ... Our spirits recovered over lunch in a rambling, hacienda-like tavern in a eucalyptus grove near the race-track. The place was bursting with cheerful Limeños: there were ponchoed Indians and prosperous Spaniards with huge cigars; it was noisy and lively and gay, and we ate delicious Peruvian kebabs dipped in blazing red sauce and washed them down with giant gins and tonic ...

Nearer to the capital there is a fine private museum of old Peruvian pottery and textiles; some of the stuffs are beautiful and a few miraculously preserved squares of fabric, woven from yellow and blue parrot feathers, are as fresh and brilliant as the day they left the forests. I *can't* care much for the pots, especially the anthropomorphic ones, it's a Toby Jug culture and one gallery is filled with earthenware vessels in the shape of fornicating couples: erotobatic stunts in elaborate postures, all of them repellently antiaphrodisiac on account of the ugliness of the little monsters concerned. A young school-master was earnestly lecturing a class of girls in front of the most energetic of these show-cases and they were scribbling industriously. Robin and I longed to know the drift of his discourse; but we were too shy to edge closer and eavesdrop. Was he holding up the exhibits as an incentive, a challenge, or a warning?

A candlelit dinner at an old Spanish palace turned into a restaurant called Las Trece Monedas ended our day.

Sartorial Note

The return to sea-level and a capital city has induced attempts at smartness. Renée is impeccable; Carl too and fully equipped to be firm with Cabinet Ministers. André is the best for all worlds: he wears a sumptuous, beautifully made suit of dark russet corduroy. End of whole suits, and on to trousers: Robin, Andrew and I have only our linen ones. Robin wears an inherited dark brown jacket and looks very elegant. Andrew wears a dashing betting-jacket of bold green plaid, extremely smart crocodile shoes, and a white silk tie with a blue pattern bought in Cuzco; I've got a tame but respectable grey tweed jacket and slightly superior gym shoes. Never mind. We all look very surprising to each other in these outfits.

LIMA   August 30

Today is the Feast of St. Rose of Lima—I love her name— so many places are shut; we didn't realize the importance of the day till too late. Understandably depressed by the panorama below the ninth-floor restaurant-window where we assemble for breakfast, Robin suggested taking yesterday's car to some- where sunny for a walk in the mountains. The roofscape is a sad one. Here and there an old Spanish house appears, with wooden *miradors* and *rejas*; there is a scattered dome or two; belfries; and the cloisters of old churches; all of them over-shadowed, held up to ridicule and outnumbered a thousand to one by a barbarous disorder of jerry-built skyscrapers. Their walls are tangled with plumbing, fissured with cracks and streaked with rust from the metal reinforcement inside the crumbling concrete. Depressing small-clothes flutter from the windows, and everything cowers under the low, damp, fidgety and watery sky.

I stayed behind to go on writing this, and to finish *The Bridge of San Luis Rey*, which I found in a bookshop last night. I last read it thirty years ago in Rumania and it reads better than ever. He obviously modelled the Marquesa de Montemayor and her daughter on Madame de Sevigné and Madame de Grignan. The Perichole (who was also used by Prosper Merimée) really existed; and the Viceroy, Don Miguel de Prat, has left many buildings and legends behind him. The only thing Wilder has got wrong is the weather. He makes Lima sound as though it basked in permanent sunshine. Otherwise, it seems unfaultable. I wish I'd brought Sachie Sitwell's book on Peru. The country is made for him.

Peru is always reminding us of authors and books. We've already had Graham Greene and Evelyn Waugh. Lima, especially today, belongs to Ronald Firbank.

An effigy of St. Rose, carried on a huge float preceded by half a dozen hooded fraternities and accompanied by a forest of banners, has been rocking slowly through the city for many hours. The Cardinal-Archbishop of Lima, a stern Spanish figure in geranium robes and overtopping by far the vast concourse that shuffled all round him, was visibly chafing at the slowness. The Cathedral slowly swallowed us all. It's a rather graceless Victorian building put up after one of the capital's many earthquakes. An ornate shrine in a side-chapel displays the skeleton of Pizarro, stabbed to death by rival Conquistadors. His palace lies just across the huge Plaza de Armas, where bull-fights are held every year. After looking at the Church of the Mercéd, whose cloister has an even longer fresco-sequence of the life of San Pedro Nolasco than the one in Cuzco, I visited the Church of Saint Rose herself. When she was a small child, she foreswore dolls as idolatrous, made a vow of chastity at the age of five, and taught mosquitoes to sing responses to the psalms instead of stinging her. She is a great favourite here, naturally enough.

The Torre-Tagle palace, not far off, is one of several Andalusian Mudéjar buildings, in fact a Sevillian nobleman's house full of fascinating, rather clumsily painted portraits of the generations of marquises who lived here: periwigged grandees in scarlet and gold lace, with marching troops and galleons crossing the background under full sail. Their great armorial coach still stands in the patio. These patrician houses are quite lost in the forest of cement monstrosities. One of them is called the Casa Pilato, like the Medinaceli palace in Seville, which it resembles in a lesser degree. If one were led blindfold from one old house to another and unbandaged and rebandaged in the nick of time, one could get a very fair impression of what a fine city old Lima must have been.

I looked at the site of the Inquisition; then had a solitary lunch in one of the many Chinese restaurants. (They are called '*chufas*', I can't discover why.[1] Many Chinese have settled on the coast, Japanese too; but I haven't consciously seen any.) It

[1] It means 'ginger' in Spanish.

was a dim, sad place, with nobody else there; the food was rather good; but it's no joke ordering Chinese food in broken Castilian ... I wrote all the afternoon in the empty bar of the Bolívar Hotel, the Ritz of Lima; then wandered about the town. The presidential palace is a post-baroque birthday-cake, guarded by sentries in scarlet breeches, spurs and plumed firemen's helmets, some of them in breast-plates, and all of them anachronistically armed with sub-machine-guns. The huge equestrian statue of Pizarro is helmeted and ostrich-plumed in full armour,[1] and liberators Bolívar and San Martín rein their bronze chargers back in tempests of mane and tail. Bells have been tolling or peeling most of the day, but none of those clangs, alas, came from the bells cast from his cannon by Pizarro's gunnery chief, my fellow-Cretan Don Pedro de Candia; his were melted back into guns in one of Peru's innumerable armed upheavals—unless, of course, they have reverted, and changed their tune yet again.

The rest of our party were back at the Alcazar. It had been a disappointing day for them except for a glimpse of Lima high-life at a country club where they had stopped for lunch. I rather envied them. I wouldn't mind seeing a few doe-eyed Latin American beauties groaning under the weight of their diamonds by the light of chandeliers.

LIMA   August 31

The great Church and Monastery of San Francisco is a splen-did ornate late Renaissance pile with galleries, patios, fine

---

[1] An identical cast stands in the plaza of Trujillo, his Estremadura birth-place.

wooden choir stalls, a tremendous frescoed cloister, a glittering chapter house and a whole roomful of putative Zurbaráns of the Evangelists and the Apostles; much more plausible Zurbaráns, indeed, than the single one which is so designated in St. Catalina's in Arequipa; but very battered and ill-kept. (A number of his pictures were sent out to the Spanish possessions.) I wonder if they *are* by him. The monastery is warrened with vaults and undercrofts, catacombs filled with the bones of dead Franciscans, rows of backbones gathered in stooks. Troops of skeletons have been plucked apart to make symmetrical patterns on the walls, rectangular baroque cartouches formed by placing rib after rib, alternately concave and convex in a wavy pattern with tilted pelvises to turn the corners. They reminded me of those avenues of dead Capuchins that we saw years ago in Palermo. I lost track of my companions in this grim labyrinth, and only caught up with them at the Alcazar an hour later.

*　　　*　　　*

We looked at the tapirs and ant-eaters and boa-constrictors in the Natural History Museum, and identified all the birds we had seen. The fauna of the Andes and the jungle were interspersed with huddled and disintegrating human mummies, one of them crouched between a bear and a panther. The only thing wrong with this wonder-house was the deafening piped music. I told one of the Indian attendants, kindly but rather severely, that the tune they were playing—*O, bella piccinina!*—was a notorious Fascist marching-song in the invasions of Abyssinia and Greece. He looked bewildered, but turned it off, and we continued in blessed silence. Robin and Andrew dawdled for ages among the trees and the flowers outside, taking compendious notes. We moved on to the vast National Museum; the most striking things there, among acres of Indian and Spanish treasures and trinkets, damascened spurs, elaborate hidalgo-ish stirrups and many canvases of the Cuzco and Arequipa schools, were some remarkable and rather beautiful seventeenth-century pictures of the Arch-angels with long fair curls; SS. Gabriel, Michael and Raphael, swaggering charmingly in feathered cavalier hats and tasselled lace collars turned down over doublets smothered in gold lace, holding long-barrelled, beautifully chased and inlaid muskets in tapering, overbred fingers: Infantes of Paradise.

In the Ethnological Museum we walked for miles. Vistas of stelae, monoliths and carved boulders dwindled interminably into the distance; we looked at a few thousand amphorae and Toby Jugs and lingered over some very interesting and sinister examples of crudely trepanned Inca skulls and other specimens of prehistoric surgery that sent a shudder through our frames. (What anaesthetics did they use? The coca-leaf?) All the same, after two hours of tramping, roller-skates or tricycles would have been welcome.

A great midday banquet interrupted all this research. Miss Beryl Griffiths, Secretary of the Andean Society, had reassembled her flock of members in Lima from a score of mountain-ranges, to make sure we caught tomorrow's aeroplane back. We were slightly dreading this feast but after we had flung a few *pisco* sours down our throats, it turned out rather fun. Our last call was at the Gold Museum, a few miles outside the town. The rooms of this hoard of Inca treasure were a glittering Aladdin's cave of every imaginable gold adornment and bauble: necklaces, rings, crowns, bracelets, collars, girdles, earrings, pendants, armlets, anklets, torques ... Many were splendid, especially the diadems and the head-dresses; but on the whole it was a shade disappointing. (When one thinks of the treasure of Mycenae! But that's not fair.) Most of the objects are made of gold rolled into sheets, cut into strips and then hammered and twisted into complicated shapes. The flimsiness reminded one, now and then, of decorations out of crackers; but exciting nevertheless. Carl naturally led the way here, peering through the glass panes with a severe and expert eye. We emerged through rooms that bristled with every kind of firearm from iron horse-pistols to elaborately wrought harquebuses fit for heavenly Infantes or archangels to shoot with. (What at? Cherubim?) The lawns outside were shaded by groves of bamboo where young deer were grazing. 'Dangerous' a notice said, but they insisted on mincing up to have their noses stroked.

When I went to scribble all this in the bar of the Bolívar, I ran into André, who was doing some last-minute shopping; so we wandered together in the swarming Calle Belén. There's not much to buy, except ponchos—I got a beauty for you in Cuzco—and horrible alpaca rugs with repoussé llamas and some rather snug llama and alpaca bedroom slippers. We bought a couple of pairs each, to carry home for our dear ones. (André and I have a secret advantage in shops where English is spoken, i.e. the Greek tongue. But we're bound to catch it one day when the *patron* turns out to be an emigré from Corinth or Kalamata.)

Back in the Alcazar, Andrew had just finished his packing, so I tackled mine. Then both had a snooze before the evening doings; dinner at the Embassy, that is to say. Renée, who can't bear *mondanités* of any kind, had dinner with André and

Carl while Robin, Andrew, Myles and I bowled off in state. Our hosts were Mr and Mrs Hugh Morgan, friends of Michael and Damaris Stewart and extremely nice. It was a large dinner and I had a charming, very quiet and very beautiful neighbour called Doña Diana de Dibos: she was English, moreover, and first married to a Spaniard who fell in the Civil War, and then—now—to a Peruvian. Exchanging life-stories, she told me she and her brother had been brought up by her father, who was a retired British admiral, half on shore and half on a yacht, at St. Tropez, when it was a little fishing town, of which her father had been affectionately styled 'the mayor' ... Suddenly I realized who she was: the sister, that is, of Mike Cumberlege, that amazing buccaneerish figure (very funny, very well read, with a single gold earring) who used to smuggle us into German-occupied Crete in little boats; he was captured later by the Germans trying to blow up the Corinth Canal, held prisoner for three years in Flossenberg concentration camp and, tragically, shot four days before the armistice: a marvellous almost mythical figure; Xan and I knew him well. His sister Diana and I fell into each other's arms and I told her lots of stories about him she'd never heard. It was too extraordinary. The Ambassadress (very pretty and animated and intelligent) is Bulgarian, though she hasn't been there since she was eight. We got into a corner and sang Bulgarian folk songs to each other, to our mutual delight and other people's possible distress. Much wine had flowed.

★   ★   ★

We are not so much upset at the thought of leaving Lima tomorrow—it's a lowering capital and such an anticlimax after all that went before; it's the thought of breaking up that we hate. These six weeks have been nothing but concord and enjoyment and exhilaration enhanced by a snowballing mythology of private jokes. Consequently, we fight for our privacy as though beleaguered by hostile tribes.

When we got back to the Alcazar, I was lured by the sound of music down a flight of stairs into a night-club; but it was so dark and sad that I felt like Ulysses among the shades, and came up again almost at once.

ON THE AEROPLANE BETWEEN LIMA AND LONDON
September 1

Early this morning, grasping our ice-axes and all of us booted once again to cut down on luggage-weight, we struggled into the street between the secret police and the tommy-gunners who were still guarding the invisible President Torres, and filled one taxi with our eight pony-loads of kit while a second bore us through the slums to the airport, under a drizzling sky. And here we are, in an aircraft entirely filled with the Andean Society. Some wear blinding ponchos and white woolly alpaca hats; some, sweatshirts stencilled with the head of Tupac Amaru, the leader of a serious Indian revolt against Spanish rule in the eighteenth century; some grasp sheaves of Quechua arrows; and some wear those wide embroidered macaroon hats like upside-down mushrooms. (No bottle-green bowlers, however.) All this gear must look a bit odd to the inhabitants, similar to a busload of Quechua Indians travelling to the Scottish Highlands in kilts and glengarries.

★   ★   ★

There is something disturbing in the faces of a few of our fellow-mountaineers, a stringy monomaniac fixity. How soon does this rictus take over? I peer covertly at the charming faces of our party. We have escaped so far.

We flew up out of the drizzle, circled over the Pacific and soared above the sunlit Andes. We were looking forward to flying over the Amazonian jungle. But, with increasing height, everything vanished in haze and cloud again. I'm on an aisle seat, scribbling this; Andrew's next door, then André, both of them reading. Carl, Renée and Robin are cleverly scattered over the two rows behind, each with a spare seat beside them for spreading their books and things. We have taken off our boots and put on lighter shoes. Gin and tonic arrived at noon, then excellent roast chicken; then, to our wonder and joy, Mouton Rothschild and Chambolles-Musigny, bottle on bottle. We flew down through the clouds in the afternoon, skimmed along the red and green cliffs of the Venezuelan coast and landed on Caracas aerodrome; but we weren't allowed out. Then the plane headed north-east over the Caribbean. Towards evening, as we lost height again, we caught fugitive glimpses of the Windward Islands: Martinique, Dominica and the cone of the Souffrière in Guadeloupe took shape through the clouds (what ages since we climbed it!). We landed in Antigua under driving rain where an official tried hard to keep us pent in the plane, but our steward stoutly insisted on our release; so we burst out and streamed across the tarmac to the ramshackle buildings where we had spent several hours on the way out. The Trades were blowing leaky convolutions of clouds overhead and the palm trees clashed their leaves as, rum punches swallowed, we boarded again helter-skelter through the downpour.

The sun set astern in crimson streaks as we boomed on eastwards. Another delicious meal arrived, and more unlimited claret and burgundy; and now, everyone is nodding off. The lights are going out one by one. Andrew and André are halfway to dreamland as Henry James and Thornton Wilder slip from their grasp ... I'll follow them soon but it won't be for long; flying eastwards, we lose many hours of the night.

Where are Alejandro and Antemio at this moment, I wonder? Fast asleep among the chair-legs and the shavings? Drinking *chicha* by the Urubamba's banks? Grazing those eight ponies and the foal on some starlit pampa? Why am I scribbling all this rot? I know perfectly well: because I feel that when I stop, the journey will be over ... We must be in mid-Atlantic by now, approaching the Azores ...... A zzzzzzzz ... (sn) ... ores ....

September 2

Dawn broke some time ago and breakfast has come and gone. Ireland streams greenly by and Cork Harbour lies just below our port wing, the pilot announces. 'Lismore!' Andrew cries, craning across André. 'Go on!' murmurs Carl from behind. Then comes the lighthouse on the south-east tip of Wexford, plainly visible. More sea follows, now Cornwall: then Hardy country: Portland Bill, green fields, the Isle of Wight. It's a clear and sunny morning, the colours are rather pale. There go a few gulls! We're flying lower and lower, the Home Counties wheel towards us, and a flashing loop of the Thames ... It'll be 'Fasten Seat Belts' soon. 'What a p-plethora of g-golf courses!' Robin says. Insatiable London looms. I'll be at Patrick's for a late breakfast in an hour's time ... It's 8 a.m.

for you; 1 a.m. in Lima. A queer kind of somnambulist elation has us all in its grip: *Heureux qui comme Ulysse a fait un beau voyage*, as one might say ... 'Extinguish cigarettes.' I thought so. Here we go.

Index

Index

INDEX

Morgan, Mr & Mrs Hugh, 105
Moyoc-Moyoc, 21, 27–8

Natar, Carl: departure from London, 4; in
    Cuzco, 9; plant-collecting, 12; nurses Indian
    boy on bus, 14; organizing arrangements, 16;
    reading, 18; reads altimeter, 24, 88; climbing,
    26, 30, 34–5, 37–9, 43, 45; conversation, 28,
    33; in camp, 33; dress, 34, 98; at Indian
    ceremony, 81–3; at Gold Museum, 104; final
    dinner in Lima, 105; on return flight, 107
Nolasco, San Pedro, *see* Pedro Nolasco, San
Ñusta, Doña Beatriz, 58

Pachacamac (Inca site), 96
Pampa Urubamba, 21
Pedro Nolasco, San, 57–8, 100
Pisac (Inca ruin), 10
pisco (drink), 17, 78, 103
Pitt-Rivers, Julian, 4
Pizarro, Francisco, 73, 97, 100–1
plants: collecting, 12, 17; unfamiliarity of, 48
Porros, Sr & Sra (of Lima), 6
Pratts (London club), 74
Prescott, W. H.: *The Conquest of Peru*, 18, 39, 43,
    96
Primavera, Hacienda, 51
Puno, 64–6, 68, 84–5

Quechua Indians: in Cuzco, 8–9; behaviour, 13–
    14; language, 18, 71; as pack-drivers, 22; dress,
    23; incuriosity and remoteness, 46; hospitality,
    50; dancing and music, 59

Rose of Lima, St., 98–100

117